The
I Can't Sing Book

THE
I Can't Sing Book

for Grownups Who
CAN'T CARRY A TUNE
in a Paper Bag
...but Want to Do Music
with Young Children

Jackie Silberg

Illustrations by Cheryl Kirk Noll

Brilliant Publications

Dedication

This book is dedicated to my parents
Bertha and Sol Silberg
who gave to me the gift of music.

I would like to thank my editor, Kathy Charner, whose clear-sighted
vision and inspired editing make my books a joy to write.

And...to Leah Curry-Rood and Larry Rood, owners of Gryphon House
Publishing who love music as much as I do and want others
to feel the same.

Published by Brilliant Publications, The Old School Yard, Leighton Road, Northall,
Dunstable LU6 2HA

Originally published in 1998 by Gryphon House, Inc, 10726 Tucker Street, Beltsville,
MD 20705, USA

Written by Jackie Silberg
Illustrated by Cheryl Kirk Noll

Typeset by Chandos Electronic Publishing, Stanton Harcourt, Oxfordshire, UK
Printed in Malta by Interprint Ltd

© Jackie Silberg 1998
ISBN 1 897675XX X

First published in the UK in 1999
10 9 8 7 6 5 4 3 2 1

The right of Jackie Silberg to be identified as author of this work has been asserted by
her in accordance with the Copyright, Designs and Patents Act 1988.

The I Can't Sing Book

Table of... Contents

Chapter 3
Music Is...Sound...39

Activities and Games That
Explore Sound 40

Chapter 4
Music Is...Language...61

Activities and Games That
Explore Language 62

Chapter 8
Music Is...Fun-filled Activities 131

Chapter 9
Music Is...A Great Way to Teach 143

Chapter 10
Music Is...Classical .149

Chapter 11
Questions Frequently Asked by Parents and Teachers 161

The I Can't Sing Book

Introduction

My earliest childhood memories are musical. Dancing lessons, singing on car trips and putting on shows for the neighbours on the front porch. When I was in the 3rd grade, Miss Keeler (one of my favourite teachers) announced that the school was going to offer piano lessons and she suggested that I might be interested. Once a week, I would take my cardboard keyboard to the auditorium and take a piano lesson. It was instant magic. My parents bought an old upright piano and I knew then that music would be in my life forever.

My parents loved music and knew hundreds of songs. When I was two years old, I could sing "The Very Thought of You", "Three Little Fishes", "When the Red, Red Robin Comes Bob, Bob, Bobbin' Along" and many, many others. Wow! What a lesson in language development!

Why should a child learn music? Ask a reading teacher who needs children to understand sequencing or a science teacher who is teaching about sound. Ask a maths teacher who understands musical time signatures or a dance instructor who needs students to understand how to count beats. Music can be used to teach maths, language and listening skills, and to help children understand science, develop coordination and develop and enhance cognitive skills in a fun and pleasurable way. Additionally, music is calming and helps us—and children—express our thoughts and emotions. It is a major form of communication.

Music also teaches spatial reasoning skills. This link is significant since spatial reasoning skills are part of the abstract reasoning skills that the brain uses to perform common, everyday activities such as walking, and complex functions, such as solving problems in mathematics and engineering.

Music is universally loved by children. Language, cultural and developmental barriers come tumbling down when children listen to sounds, sing songs, discover rhythms and patterns in nature, make instruments and listen to music. Music is non-judgmental. There is no right or wrong. It is what it is. Everyone can be successful in music.

Music is a gift. It will enrich your life and will always be your friend. When you hear a child singing to himself before he goes to sleep or humming as he builds his tower of blocks, you know that music is becoming his friend too.

Music Is... for Everyone

Life is filled with music, whether it is the song of a bird, the clacking of wheels on a train or songs on a radio. While everyone enjoys music, it is important to know what children at different developmental levels enjoy and understand. The following is a brief outline of the typical pattern of music development in young children. Remember that children of all ages benefit from musical experiences and that what children enjoy as toddlers they may still enjoy as three year olds.

Infants will respond to music in their surroundings. Research has shown that babies respond to music while in the womb. Holding an infant while singing is a wonderful gift. The newborn feels the vibrations of the human body at the same time he hears the singing. When an infant begins to babble and discovers his voice, he will be amazed at all of the wonderful sounds that he can make.

Toddlers enjoy jumping and running to music. Shakers (bottles or unbreakable jars filled with beans or other materials, see page 105) and sticks (short ones!) are wonderful instruments for toddlers. They develop fine motor skills and give toddlers an opportunity to explore musical sounds. If you play music for toddlers, they will rock back and forth and jump up and down, showing remarkable energy.

Two year olds enjoy movement games (see pages 73–85), singing and fingerplays such as The Announcement Song, page 62, Incy Wincy Spider, page 63, Chanting Games and Magic Word, pages 64–65 and Where Is Thumbkin, page 62. Two year olds can begin to sing simple songs and can usually fill in one or two words of a song.

Three year olds delight in using rhythm instruments (see pages 104–129). They enjoy exploring the variety of sounds they can make with the instruments. They love songs with actions, call and response songs, and they particularly like making loud and soft sounds. Three year olds enjoy listening to songs, clapping hands and stamping feet. They love musical games (see pages 77, 78, 81) that involve galloping, jumping, walking and simple dancing to music.

Four year olds are enthusiastic and dramatic, and they love silly sounds, silly words and silly songs. This precious age will march, dance, sing, act out songs and make up their own songs as they begin to match sounds and tones. Four year olds can play simple games like "Hokey Cokey" and can play most rhythm instruments. This is also the perfect age to introduce classical music.

Five year olds (and older children, too)

love all kinds of musical activities. They can play simple rhythm instruments in a very sophisticated way. Five year olds enjoy attending musical events. Singing is something they do all day long, often making up their own songs about what they do throughout the day. Singing call and response songs and making up songs are favourite things to do with five year olds. Clapping to rhythms and imitating rhythms are two sophisticated music skills this age can master.

The activities and games in this book develop music skills and music appreciation in all of the above age levels. At the same time, these activities and games encourage children's developing listening, language, motor and cognitive skills and enhance self-esteem.

Family Music

Singing is a wonderful way to build special, loving relationships with your children. You can even sing to your baby while he is in the womb. Research tells us that babies can hear during the last few months of pregnancy, so this is a perfect time for mothers and fathers to take time to relax and sing to your baby. Some people even place megaphones on their stomachs when they sing to their unborn child. Studies have shown that if you sing the same song to your baby in the womb, he will recognize the melody after he is born.

After the baby is born, hold him and sing to him, stimulating all of his senses. He hears your voice, he sees your face, he smells your body and feels your vibrations as you sing.

As your children grow, develop special songs and rituals. Families enjoy making up songs about special events, pets or just a bunch of silly words. It's fun to do this with familiar tunes because the children know the tune. Riding in the car, taking a bath and going to sleep are all times that songs can enrich. Bedtime with a story and a lullaby is a time to relax together. Many families have special songs for each child, sometimes made-up songs with which the child strongly identifies for a lifetime. These family songs are a never-ending part of a family; neither time nor distance affects them. They are present in children's hearts at two years old and at eighteen years old. They are part of your life in England, Ireland, Scotland, Wales or across an ocean. It's a bond that never disappears.

In today's busy world, many children don't see their relatives very often. Songs about grandparents, favourite aunts and uncles are reminders during and after a visit with that family member. These songs can be popular songs you hear on the radio, a classic song (perhaps you sang "She'll Be Comin' 'Round the Mountain" while waiting for Aunt Jean's train, bus or plane to arrive) or a song you made up for a particular relative.

Following a family concert last year, a parent came to me and said, "My father always said that you can sing until you die!" Think about it! It's worth passing on to your children.

Lullabies

Lullabies are warm, tender and gentle songs for everyone: infants, toddlers, preschoolers, grandparents, pets, and anyone else who needs to be comforted. Gentle rocking, soft humming and the close warmth of a loved one's voice are used throughout the world to comfort and reassure a restless child.

Once a child is too large to rock to sleep in one's arms, a reassuring lullaby still can be an important part of the bedtime ritual—the transition from the active to the quiet part of the day, a time to talk and sing and read. It is a great opportunity for bonding and back rubs; children (and adults) need loving strokes. Once established, this very personal time can extend right into your child's teen years, its shape adapting as the child's needs change, eventually becoming an opportunity for conversation.

What is a lullaby? Musicologists believe that the first ones were charms and spells that were changed and sung by parents to protect their children from the demons of the night. Lullabies have soothing rhythms, supportive messages and beautiful imagery.

Rock-A-Bye Baby

**Rock a bye baby
On the treetop.
When the wind blows
The cradle will rock.
When the bough breaks
The cradle will fall,
And down will come
baby
Cradle and all.**

This most beloved of lullabies was written by an American, Effie I. Crockett. Effie was only fifteen when, in 1887, she was a babysitter for a restless child. To lull the child to sleep, she improvised a melody and varied the words from an old Mother Goose rhyme, "Hush-a-bye on the tree-top". Some time later she sang the tune for her music teacher, who, in turn, recommended the song to a Boston publisher. Effie gave her permission for publication, but fearing her father's disapproval, she had it published under her grandmother's name, "Canning". Only after the song began to sweep the country did Effie tell her father that she wrote it.

Making up a lullaby

● Pick three or four words that pertain to your child including his name. For example, "Night, night, Shaun, Shaun, nighty night."
● Say these words over and over and soon you will find yourself singing the words instead of just saying them.
● Try singing the music that you hear with the words. Don't worry if it changes each time you sing it. That's normal!
● Hold your child in your arms and rock him back and forth. Say or sing the words you've just made up.
● Encourage your child to hold a doll or stuffed animal in his arms and sing a lullaby.
● After you have sung your lullaby a few times, try changing the first letter of the word "night". For example, "sight, sight, Shaun" or "might, might, Mhaun".
● This will get kind of silly (especially with five year olds) but it is a great language developer.

• Other familiar lullabies include:
   Hush Little Baby
   All the Pretty Horses
   All Through the Night
   Sleep, Baby, Sleep
   Star Light, Star Bright

Music is one of the seven areas of intelligence, and it uses some of the other six components. Songs are linguistic, rhythm is logical, dance and finger manipulation on instruments is body kinaesthetic, musical interpretation is interpersonal and the connection between musicians and instruments can be intrapersonal.

chapter 2

Music Is... Rhythm

Children begin feeling and sensing rhythmic patterns at a very early age. A parent told me, "My baby adores music. Whenever I sing to her or play music, she jumps up and down in her cot, coos, dances, smiles and giggles." I have heard this and similar remarks over and over for many years. And it's true! Children do respond to music. For them, it's as natural as walking and talking. From infancy, as babies develop, the sounds of rattles and musical toys intrigue them. Toddlers begin composing their own rhythmic patterns by banging on saucepans and other surfaces. A tune on the radio or television can inspire a child to respond spontaneously by swaying and bouncing her little body.

Rhythm is something that happens over and over again in the same way. It is a pattern that repeats itself. A room can have a rhythm in the way the windows or ceiling follow a pattern.

Clothes can have a rhythm in the way the stripes or dots follow a pattern. Seasons have a rhythm: winter, spring, summer, autumn. Night and day happen over and over again. Rhythmic experiences are a vital part of everyday life. When we begin to understand the rhythm of the world, we begin to understand ourselves. There is rhythm and order in beauty.

Activities and Games That Explore Rhythm

Fast and Slow ♪ 2+

TEACHES ABOUT FAST AND SLOW RHYTHMS

- Hold your arms straight out from your body. Make little circles with your hands, very slowly at first, then a little faster, faster still, then very fast.
- Repeat this movement and ask your child to copy you.
- Now, hold out your fingers. Bend them and straighten them. First very slowly, then a little faster.
- Repeat this movement and ask your child to copy you.
- Keep moving different parts of your body slowly, then faster—your head, your shoulders, your feet (sitting or lying on your back), etc.
- Always repeat the movements and have your child copy you.
- Ask your child to move across the room in different ways. Discuss whether this is a fast way or slow way.
- Walk, run, hop, skip and jump; cross the room fast and return slowly.

The I Can't Sing Book

Rhythm in Nature 2+

TEACHES OBSERVATION OF RHYTHM PATTERNS IN NATURE

- Practically everything in the world behaves according to its own rhythmic pattern. The seasons change, day changes into night, green leaves change to many colours, ocean and radio waves move according to certain frequencies.
- Go on a rhythm outing. Look for patterns in leaves, flowers, rock formations and clouds.
- Experiment with different kinds of movement. As the surface you are walking on changes, change your movement. Hop on the grass, tiptoe on concrete, stamp your feet on the earth.
- Observing the world and its rhythms will help young minds find order in the world.

Rhythm of the Rain 2+

TEACHES ABOUT RHYTHM AND THE SOUNDS OF NATURE

- This creative, dramatic game involves body movement. It is very effective in creating a mood.
- Say the following words:

> Rain, rain, go away.
> Come again another day.
> Everybody wants to play. (or substitute a child's name for "everybody")

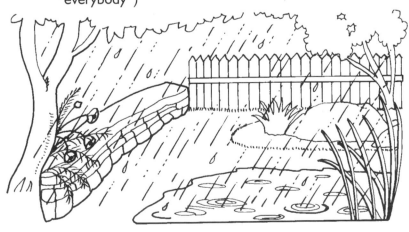

- If you know the melody of this song, you can sing it too.
- Sing or say the words again and do the following actions.

> Make soft raindrops—snap your fingers softly
> Make louder raindrops—snap louder
> Make very loud raindrops—slap your hands on your thighs
> Make thunder—stamp your feet
> Make lightning—clap your hands sharply

- Now reverse the procedure until you have come back to the soft raindrops again.

Winter Rhythms

TEACHES ABOUT THE RHYTHMS IN NATURE

- There are many rhythm patterns in nature. The changing of the seasons, night and day, the chirping of birds and ocean waves. There is also rhythm in snow falling.
- Snow has been a recurring theme in art. Frederick Chopin composed music about snow. Ralph Waldo Emerson, Robert Frost and many other poets have written poetry using snow as a theme. Many artists such as Pieter Breughel painted pictures with snow scenes. This didn't happen by accident. Snow is a moving and rhythmic force of nature.
- Talk about snow with your child. Can you hear snow falling? How does snow feel? How does snow smell? Does snow fall straight down or does it swirl around as it falls?
- Create snow by tearing white paper into very small pieces. Get up high and drop the "snow". Watch how it falls. Do this several times and continue the discussion about how the snow falls. (Organize a snow removal crew because you will have lots of paper on the floor.)
- Pretend to be snowflakes. Whirl, twirl and fall to the ground. What else falls softly like the snow? Feathers and leaves and what else?

● Act out the following poem:

> Snowflakes, snowflakes
> Whirling, twirling,
> Snowflakes, snowflakes all around.
> Snowflakes, snowflakes
> Whirling, twirling,
> Falling softly to the ground.

This Is the Way

TEACHES LANGUAGE AND RHYTHM

● This lovely rhythm chant is one that children enjoy very much because the rhythm of the words is a lot of fun.

> This is the way the ladies ride
> A clippety clop, a clippety clop
> And a clippety, clippety, clippety clop.
>
> This is the way the gentlemen ride,
> A gallop a trot, a gallop a trot
> And a gallop, a gallop, a gallop a trot.
>
> This is the way the farmers ride
> A hobblety hop, a hobblety hop
> And a hobblety, hobblety, hobblety hop.
>
> This is the way the firefighters ride,
> A clangety clang, a clangety clang
> And a clangety, clangety, clangety clang.

● Add your own verses.

> This is the way the police officers ride—make a siren sound
> This is the way the pilots ride—make an aeroplane sound
> This the way the train conductors ride—make a train sound

- The rhythm of this chant is contagious. As you say it over and over you will begin to feel it throughout your entire body.
- Add movement with the words. You can gallop for clippety clop, pretend to ring a bell as you run for clangety clang.
- Play rhythm instruments for the different sounds.

Be a Rhythm   3+

DEVELOPS AWARENESS OF RHYTHM PATTERNS

- Listen to a rhythm pattern with your child (a clock, for example). Pretend to be a clock and make a sound each time the clock ticks.
- Put your child's hand on her heart or on your heart. Feel the rhythm of the heart. Make a sound for each heartbeat.
- Pretend to be a frog. Hop around the room. Say the word "rivet" in a steady pattern.
- Talk about things that have fast or slow rhythms. Be a fast buzzing bee or a slow tortoise.

The I Can't Sing Book

Everyday Rhythms

3+

- There is rhythm all around us. Teaching children to observe this rhythm helps them to be aware of themselves and the environment.
- Talk with your child about the different kinds of work that people do—cooking, driving a car, washing dishes, picking up toys, talking on the phone and writing letters.
- Act out some of these rhythms with your child. Say the words describing what you are doing in a rhythmic way—"cooking eggs, cooking eggs" or "turn the wheel, turn the wheel".
- Choose a rhythm that you would like to act out and say the following poem.

> Work a rhythm, work a rhythm, work a rhythm now.
> Work a rhythm, work a rhythm, I will show you how.

- Act out the rhythm that you have chosen.

Rhythm Robot

3+

TEACHES RHYTHM

- Make up a sound as you move one arm in and out. For example, blip, blip, blip. Your child will have wonderful ideas for sounds.
- Make up a different sound as you walk in a steady beat. Maybe, gook, gook, gook.
- Try walking and make the walking sound, then stop and move your arm to the arm sound.
- You can make up sounds for many different moving parts— nodding your head, sticking out your tongue (a favourite) and moving your elbows in and out.

Follow the Beat

3+

- This game requires a beeping timer or a metronome.
- Let your child tap a stick on the floor to the rhythm that is beeping.
- A metronome is particularly nice because you can change the speed of the beat.
- Pretend to be different animals and change the kind of animal as the beat changes. A slow beat could be an elephant, a medium beat goes nicely with a kangaroo and a fast beat is good for a squirrel.

The Clock Game

3+

- The rhythm of a clock is a good sound to imitate because the beat of the clock is very steady. This helps young children develop an awareness of a steady beat.
- Listen to a clock and move with the beat. Start by moving your index finger back and forth in time with the ticking that you hear. This takes a lot of concentration; the louder the tick, the easier it is to hear.
- Keep adding body parts. Keep moving your index finger and at the same time move your head from side to side to the beat.
- Next, sway your entire body to the steady beat.

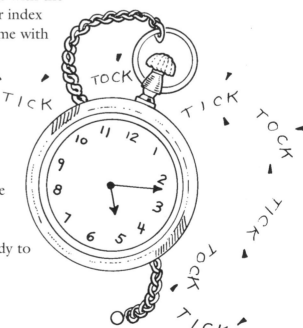

The I Can't Sing Book

Rhythm Variations

● Hold your child's hand and tell her you are both going to be different kinds of rhythms.
● Here are some of the rhythms that you can try.

> Bumpy—jump on both feet in a circle
> Smooth—glide your feet as if you are skating
> Straight—walk with your feet directly in front of one another
> Soft—walk on tiptoe
> Fast—walk very fast
> Slow—walk slowly
> Strong—march with stamping feet
> Zigzag—zigzag around the room

● Try doing all of the rhythms in a circle or a triangle.
● You can also play recorded music as you play this game.

I Use My Brain

ENHANCES SELF-CONCEPT

● Play this rhythmical fingerplay with children.

> I use my brain to think, think, think. (touch your head with
>   your index finger)
> I use my nose to smell. (touch your nose)
> I use my eyes to blink, blink, blink. (blink your eyes)
> And I use my mouth to YELL. (yell)
> I use my mouth to giggle, giggle, giggle. (touch your mouth)
> I use my hips to bump. (sway your hips)
> I use my toes to wiggle, wiggle, wiggle. (wiggle your toes)
> And I use my legs to jump. (jump)
>   Jackie Silberg

- Additional ideas for playing this rhythm game.

> Clap the rhythm of the poem. Notice that the rhythm is the same every other line.
> Clap two lines and speak two lines.
> Clap two lines and stamp two lines.

Rhythm Everywhere 3+

TEACHES ABOUT RHYTHM

- Young children love to say new words. They often will repeat the same word over and over simply because they enjoy saying it.
- Choose a favourite word like "pizza" and try saying it with different parts of your body.

> Say it with your hands—clap to the syllables
> Say it with your head—move your head to the syllables
> Say it with your feet—stamp the syllables
> Say it with your eyes—blink your eyes to the syllables

- Try adding a second word and say it many ways.
- Now play a game of clapping or tapping or nodding one of your child's favourite words and see if your child can guess the word.
- This is a fun game to play with favourite song titles. Tap the first line of "Mary Had a Little Lamb" on your child's back.

Research has identified rhythm as a factor in learning, language development and memory. Young children enjoy nursery rhymes, like to have patterns repeated and respond rhythmically to music.

The I Can't Sing Book

Listen for the Rhythm   3+

- Children enjoy imitating sounds. How often have you heard them imitate train whistles, police sirens or aeroplanes when they are at play? Many of these sounds have rhythm patterns that can be easily identified and imitated.
- Listen to sounds with your child, like those of a ticking clock, windscreen wipers or dripping water. Try imitating these sounds in a steady rhythm pattern.
- Play a game with your child by making one of the sounds you were imitating and see if she can guess which rhythm sound you are making. Ask your child to do the same and you can guess the sound.

Hand and Body Jive   3+

Hand and body jive is a way of expressing rhythmic music with your hands or your body. It's similar to a fingerplay or actions that go with songs. Here are some examples:

Miss Polly Had a Dolly

Miss Polly had a dolly that was sick, sick, sick. (look at a pretend doll in your arms)

So she called for the doctor to come quick, quick, quick. (dial a telephone)

The doctor came with his bag and his hat. (tip your hat)

And he knocked on the door with a rat-a-tat-tat. (knock on the door)

The doctor looked at dolly and he shook his head (shake head slowly and sadly)

And he said, "Miss Polly, put her right to bed." (shake your finger)

He wrote out a paper for a pill, pill, pill. (pretend to write)

"I'll be back in the morning, yes I will, will, will." (wave goodbye)

Hambone, hambone, where you been? (Repeat)
Round the world and back again. (Repeat)
Hambone, hambone, that's no name. (Repeat)
I still answer just the same. (Repeat)

Clap your hands rhythmically as you say the words. Try alternating clapping your hands and clapping on your knees. This is a popular rhyme from the Appalachian mountains.

Whoops, Baby

Take your child's hand in yours. Starting with the little finger, touch the tip of each finger as you say the word "baby". When you get to the word "whoops", you will be on the index finger. Slide down the index finger and slide up the thumb. Say, "baby" when you get to the tip of the thumb. Then a second "whoops" up to the index finger. Continue back to the little finger with the word "baby".

Baby, baby, baby, baby, whoops baby, whoops baby, baby, baby, baby.

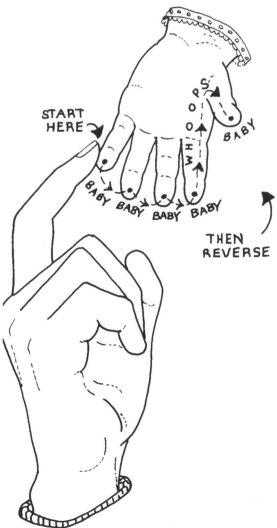

START HERE

WHOOPS

BABY

BABY BABY BABY BABY

THEN REVERSE

Miss Mary Mack

3+

● "Miss Mary Mack" is a traditional American skipping rope chant and very popular with young children. The rhythm of the chant seems to have a special appeal for children and they will respond to the words with lots of body movement.

> Miss Mary Mack, Mack, Mack
> All dressed in black, black, black
> With silver buttons, buttons, buttons
> Up and down her back, back, back.
>
> She asked her mother, mother, mother
> For fifteen pence, pence, pence
> To see the elephants, elephants, elephants
> Jump over the fence, fence, fence.
> They jumped so high, high, high.
> They reached the sky, sky, sky
> And they didn't come back, back, back
> Till the fourth of July, ly, ly.

● Say the words with your child several times.
● Say the words and leave out the last word that repeats three times.
● Substitute words with claps. Miss Mary (clap, clap, clap), all dressed in (clap, clap, clap).
● When you are clapping the words, whisper the words at the same time.
● Once you can say the poem and express the rhythm with claps, try using rhythm instruments instead of clapping.

Tick Tock

TEACHES A STEADY BEAT

- Children feel the steady beat of rhythmic sounds.
- A clock is a wonderful way to listen to a steady beat.
- Give your child a clock (one with a loud beat) and ask her to listen to it. Then ask her to clap her hands to the tick tock of the clock.
- Now try clapping hands without the clock.
- Give your child two rhythm sticks or two wooden spoons to hit together.
- Start the "tick tock" sound and sing a song as you hit the rhythm.
- Songs with a steady rhythm include:
  - Are you sleeping?
  - Yankee doodle
  - Twinkle, twinkle little star

I Can Feel the Rhythm   4+

TEACHES AWARENESS OF SELF

- We all have our very own individual rhythms within our bodies. Show your child where her heart is. Put her hands on her heart and let her listen to the steady, rhythmical beat.
- Ask her questions about what she hears. "Is your heart beat even, slow, fast?" Use words that your child will understand.
- Now, show your child where her pulse is. This is a little harder to find. On the wrist or the neck are usually the easiest places.
- The pulse and the heartbeat are reflections of the heart's activity, pumping blood through the body and bringing oxygen and food to the cells. Explain as much as your child will understand.
- Sing the following song to the tune of "The farmer's in his den".

> The rhythm of my heart, the rhythm of my heart
> Boom, boom, di boom di boom
> The rhythm of my heart.
>
> The rhythm of my pulse, the rhythm of my pulse
> Boom, boom, di boom, di boom
> The rhythm of my pulse.

Rhythm in the Room   **4+**

TEACHES ABOUT RHYTHM PATTERNS IN THE ENVIRONMENT

- Rhythms are a part of daily life. This game will reinforce the definition of rhythm for your child.
- Look at the walls. Notice the rhythm of panelling, of window panes or blinds or curtains.
- Look at the floor. Do you see a rhythmic pattern in the carpet or wood?
- Look at the ceiling. Does it have a pattern?
- Clothes have a rhythm. Look at the stripes, floral patterns, dots and checks on your clothes.

Art Rhythms   **4+**

EXPRESSING RHYTHM PATTERNS IN ART

- Children learn through active participation. Expressing rhythm patterns in art is not only a way to learn the concept of rhythm, it is a way to understand order, organization and discipline.
- Draw a simple design on a large piece of paper. Start with something simple like a circle or a curvy line. Make the same design all over the paper. Point out that the same pattern has been used over and over.
- Encourage your child to create a rhythm picture.

Music Is...Rhythm

- Another way to form patterns is to cut shapes from construction paper and paste them in patterns.
- Also try using buttons, beads or shells to make patterns on paper. This gives your rhythm picture three dimensions. You can feel the patterns with your fingers.

Days of the Week 4+

LEARNING THE DAYS OF THE WEEK

- The days of the week all have the same number of syllables except Saturday.
- Clap your hands to the words: Monday, Tuesday, Wednesday, Thursday, Friday (all have two claps), Saturday (three claps) and Sunday (two claps.)
- Some variations on this game are:

   Say the days and clap "Saturday".
   Say the days in a soft voice and say "Saturday" in a big voice.
   Clap the days and stamp your feet on the word "Saturday".
   Clap the days and say the word "Saturday".
   Stamp your feet for the days and say the word "Saturday".

Your Name Is a Rhythm 4+

TEACHES RECOGNIZING AND COMPARING THE SAME

AND DIFFERENT RHYTHMS

- Tell your child that her name is very special and has its very own rhythm. Say your child's name and clap your hands on each syllable of her name.

   Jill Weston
   / / /   ("/" means to clap)

- Now say your name and clap your hands on each syllable of your name.

   Vickie Weston
   / / / /

The I Can't Sing Book

- Now, clap Jill's name and ask your child if she can tell which name you are clapping. Then, clap your name and ask your child if she knows whose name you are clapping.
- Listening to the rhythm and actually clapping the rhythm are two very different activities; the latter may be hard for your young child to do.
- A nice game to play is to clap the first name with one part of the body and the second name with a different body part. Clap "Jill" with your hands and stamp your feet for "Weston". Can you think of some other combinations?

Talking Rhythm

TEACHES COMMUNICATION USING SOUND AND RHYTHM

- What are some ways that you can make sounds with your body?

> Hands—clap, slap, beat chest
> Feet—stamp, jump
> Fingers—snap
> Voice—talk, sing, hum, moan, bark, howl
> Mouth—blow, sigh, click, whistle

- Choose a rhyme or song that your child likes to say. "Twinkle, twinkle, little star" is a good one to try.
- Clap to the syllables as you say the words "Twinkle, twinkle, little star".

- Help your child clap and say the next line "How I wonder what you are".
- After you have done this a few times, try clapping and just moving your mouth to the words as you clap.
- Continue as long as your child is enjoying the game. Try using different parts of your body.
- Soon you will be able to use different parts of your body to express the song.

I've Got a Rhythm 4+

DEVELOPS LISTENING SKILLS

- Say the following poem.

> I've got a rhythm.
> Listen to my rhythm.
> I've got a rhythm.
> Can you do it too?
>> Jackie Silberg

- Say a simple word five times in an even, steady rhythm.

    dog, dog, dog, dog, dog

- Ask your child to say the word with you.
- Now, clap your hands each time you say the word and ask your child to join you.

    clap, clap, clap, clap, clap

- Say the above poem. When you ask "Can you do it too?" clap five times with an even, steady beat. Ask your child to copy you.
- Express the rhythm with other body actions such as snapping fingers, clicking tongues and jumping in the air.
- Try animal sounds such as dogs barking and ducks quacking to express the rhythm.

The I Can't Sing Book

An Accent Game

DEVELOPS LISTENING SKILLS

- One important element of music that is related to rhythm is the accent. This gives meaning to music and often suggests a particular mood or thought.
- Experiment with your child. Sing a familiar song and try accenting the last word of each line. Notice how the entire idea can change or even lose its meaning.
- The song "Twinkle, twinkle, little star" would sound different if you accented the last word of each line.
- With older children, sing a familiar song and ask them which words have the accents. A good rule of thumb is that in a song, usually the first or second word in a line will be accented.

One, Two, Three, Cow   4+

RESPONDING TO RHYTHM PATTERN

- The object of this game is to learn to say a word on the beat. It is a wonderful rhythm lesson.
- Play the game with animal names or other subjects that are familiar to your child.

Music Is...Rhythm

- Clap your hands together four times saying the number as you clap.

One   Two   Three Four
Clap   Clap   Clap   Clap

- Try to clap in a steady, even rhythm. Keep clapping over and over as you count up to four each time. Don't stop in between four and one.
- When you and your child are clapping in a steady rhythm, substitute the word "cow" for the number four. You will be clapping and saying "one, two, three, cow".
- Your goal is to clap and say the name of an animal on the number four.
- If you or your child should miss a beat, keep going and say an animal's name on the next group of four.

Ring the Bell

DEVELOPS A RHYTHMIC BEAT

- Say the word "ding" and hold it for four counts (count one, two, three, four).
- To show how long to hold the sound, swing your arm back and forth for the four counts.
- Repeat the same thing while saying the word "dong".
- Now try "ding" for two arm swings and "dong" for two arm swings.
- This is a wonderful way to begin to teach rhythm to young children. You can also play this game with a child's name. For example, with the name "Mary" there are two arm swings for "Ma" and two arm swings for "ry".
- If a name is one syllable like James, say the word and hold it for four arm swings.

Music stimulates the portion of the brain nearest to the maths and spatial centres.

The I Can't Sing Book

A Rhythm Round

DEVELOPS A TOTAL SENSE OF RHYTHM

- This group game can be played with children as young as four and can be adapted to any subject.
- Find a subject that is familiar to the children and elicit vocabulary from them. For example, talk about spring. Words that might be used are warm weather, birds, grass or flowers.
- Choose three words that have been discussed: birds, grass, flowers.
- Now you can have a "rhythm round". A round is a musical form where several groups sing different parts of a song at the same time. "Row, row, row your boat" is a good example.
- Divide the children into three groups. Assign a word to each child (or group if there are more than three children) and ask them to repeat the word four times.

> birds, birds, birds, birds
> grass, grass, grass, grass
> flowers, flowers, flowers, flowers

- After the children have practised their parts, begin the round. The first child begins by saying "birds" four times. She then repeats the word again four times. She will keep repeating the word four times over and over. Once you start, don't stop!
- While the word "birds" is being said, instruct the next child to start the word "grass", then the next child starts with the word "flowers".
- When all three children are chanting at the same time, there will be lots of fun for everyone.
- If you find that three words are too many, try the game with two words for two children or two groups.

Music is a gift. It will enrich your life and will always be your friend. When you hear a child singing to himself before he goes to sleep or humming as he builds his tower of blocks, you know that music is becoming his friend too.

Music is therapeutic. It can relax children and calm them down for quieter activities. It can soothe hurt feelings and turn tears to smiles. Music can also be a very effective and positive way to discipline, change attitudes and promote social interaction among children.

chapter 3

Music Is...
Sound

C lose your eyes right now and listen to the sounds around you. Can you identify what you hear? It takes a lot of focus and concentration, doesn't it? Recognizing sounds and learning how to distinguish sounds are essential skills in music. Children's hearing develops while they are still in the womb. Infants concentrate on the sounds they hear and begin to differentiate and respond differently to the various sounds. An infant will babble one way to one sound and babble differently to another sound. As children grow, their ability to recognize and distinguish sounds develops. The games and activities in this chapter teach sound awareness and discrimination, and they also develop listening skills.

Activities and Games That Explore Sound

Awareness of Sounds $1\frac{1}{2}^{+}$

TEACHES ABOUT SOUNDS IN THE ENVIRONMENT

- An awareness of environmental sounds connects us to our world.
- Some of the everyday environmental sounds that we hear include wind, fire engines, dogs barking, alarm clocks, doors slamming, car horns and train whistles. Can you add to this list?
- Try imitating some of these sounds with your child. Once you have done this a few times, make one of the sounds and ask your child to guess which sound you made. Reverse the process and guess one of your child's sounds.
- What are some other sounds you can make? Knock on the door, call on the telephone, whistle, tap on the window.
- Play the same game again, guessing each other's sounds.

What Do You Hear? 2^{+}

DEVELOPS LISTENING SKILLS

- These games teach young children to listen carefully and develop a sense of tone.
- Fill separate containers with marbles, sand, sticks of wood and other objects that make a distinctive sound.
- Fill two of each kind of sound maker. Start with three sets, eg, two containers of marbles, two of sand and two with sticks.
- Pick up one of the containers and shake it. Ask your child to find another that sounds the same.
- Arrange the containers from the softest sound to the loudest sound. After your child has listened to this order a few times, mix up the containers and let your child try putting them in order from the softest to the loudest sound.

The I Can't Sing Book

Tape Recorder Games 2+

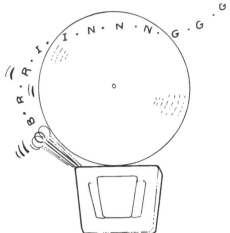

- Pre-record four or five common sounds like a doorbell ringing, a clock ticking, water running, etc.
- Play the sounds and ask your child to identify them.
- Pre-record sounds that take place in a particular place — the doorbell, typing on a computer keyboard, water running.
- Ask your child to identify the sound and tell you where the sound can be found.

Let's Take a Walk 2+

ENCOURAGES AN AWARENESS OF SOUNDS

IN THE ENVIRONMENT

- There are hundreds of sounds that we hear every day. Many of these sounds are faint and indistinct; often we do not even notice them. This game helps children tune in to the world around them.
- Take a walk outdoors with your child. Tell him that you are going to listen for different sounds. Sounds you might listen for: wind blowing, dogs barking, birds chirping, cars driving by, bird conversations (and other animal conversations), people talking, bees and other insects buzzing and lawn mowers.
- Pick one sound and listen for it with your child. When you hear that sound, choose another sound to listen for.
- Get down on the grass and listen to the earth. You will hear earth sounds and other sounds.
- Walk on different surfaces and listen to the sounds. Take off your shoes and walk barefoot. Notice the different sounds that your feet make with and without shoes.

Music Is...Sound

Popcorn 2⁺

- Popcorn is an excellent tool for demonstrating the concept of sound versus silence.
- Pop corn and observe with your child that at first there is no noise and as the kernels begin to pop, it gets noisier and noisier.
- A see-through popper is fascinating to watch and listen to.
- Pretend that you are a popcorn kernel and imitate the sounds that you heard, starting with one pop and ending with lots and lots of pops.

Mouth Trumpets 2⁺

TEACHES ABOUT MOUTH SOUNDS

- Pretend you are playing the trumpet.
- Play the music that they play at sporting events, such as football matches.
- Help your child pretend to do the same.
- Play the fanfare and pretend to introduce different people.
- Play the fanfare and say "Ladies and Gentlemen, may I present (child's name)."
- You can introduce pets, relatives and friends or inanimate objects.

The Toothbrush Game 2⁺

TEACHES GOOD HEALTH HABITS

- Play this game with your child. You will have a lot of fun and get your teeth clean at the same time.
- At tooth brushing time sing the following to the tune of "Row, Row, Row Your Boat".

> Brush, brush, brush your teeth,
> Round and round and round.
> Brushing, brushing, brushing, brushing
> What a lovely sound.

- On the third line, in place of the words "brushing, brushing, brushing, brushing", just listen to the brushing sound.

The I Can't Sing Book

Body Sounds

3⁺

- Before there were pianos and guitars, people made sounds with their bodies.
- Think of the different parts of your body that can make a sound.
- Rubbing—hands together, hands on different surfaces, toes against the floor.
- Slapping—open hands against your chest; slapping your thighs, bottom, stomach and hard surfaces.
- Snapping—fingers and toes.
- Tapping—with fingertips, nails, heels and toes on different objects.
- Clapping—hands together or against someone else's hands.
- Mouth sounds—clicking teeth together, gargling, smacking your lips, popping your cheeks and slapping puffed up cheeks.

Lip Bubbles

3⁺

JUST FOR FUN

- Take your index finger and pull it over your lips starting at the top and moving downward.
- As you are moving your finger across your lips, make a humming sound. You will hear the "bubble" sound.
- Say the following poem and instead of saying the word "bubble" make a lip bubble.

Bubble, said the kettle.
Bubble, said the pot.
Bubble, bubble, bubble
We are very, very hot.

Music Is...Sound

Waa Waas   3⁺

- Say "waaaaaaaaaaaa". As you are making the sound, move your palm on and off your mouth.
- Brass instruments often use a mute to make this sound. The player puts a mute (something to stop up the bell) and then moves the mute in and out of the instrument.

Whispering   3⁺

DEVELOPS AN AWARENESS OF VOICE CONTROL

- Whispering is very hard for young children because they haven't learned to modulate their voices. They are usually not aware of how their own voice sounds.
- Set aside a few minutes to practise whispering.
- Try whispering animal sounds. This is great fun and your child will love it.

Loud and Soft Sounds   3⁺

DEVELOPS CONCEPT OF LOUD AND SOFT

- Talk about your ears with your child. Touch them and count them.
- Put your hands over your ears and talk. Point out the difference in the sound when your ears are covered.
- Talk about animal sounds. Which animals make loud sounds and which ones make soft sounds? Which animals make both loud and soft sounds?
- Ask your child to make a loud cow sound, a soft duck sound, etc.
- Play music and turn the music player louder and softer. Each time you change the sound, ask your child to identify if it is loud or soft.
- Try doing other things loudly or softly, such as walking, chewing, singing.

Looking for Sounds 3⁺

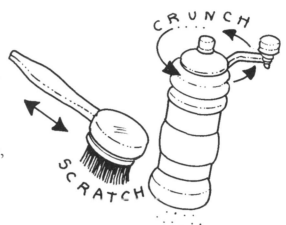

This game is like a scavenger hunt. Talk about all the different kinds of sounds you can listen to and try to find examples of these sounds.

Crunchy, funny, terrible, scary, scratchy, buzzing, humming, a sound that stops or, perhaps, metal sounds.

The kitchen is a good place to find things that make these sounds.

With younger children, start with two or three sounds. Look around and when you find an object that makes the sound, take it to the table.

Pick up the object, make the sound and give the descriptive word.

Pick a few objects and take them to the table. Tell your child to pick up the object that makes a scary sound, a crunchy sound, etc.

Match the Tones 3⁺

When young children practise recognizing the differences in sounds, they pave the way for clarity of speech.

Put three objects on a table: a block, a book and a ball. If you use objects that all start with the same letter, you are also helping to develop recognition of beginning sounds.

Ask your child, "Where is the book?" Your child picks up the book and answers, "Here is the book." Continue, asking the same question about the block and the ball.

When you have played the game a few times, change your voice when asking the question. Ask your child to answer you in the same kind of voice that you use.

Different voices that you can use include loud, soft, whisper, sweet, gruff, hold your nose, fast and slow.

Music Is...Sound

Animal Singing   3+

DEVELOPS CREATIVITY AND THINKING SKILLS

- Pick a favourite song and sing it with your child. Maybe, "The wheels on the bus" or "This old man".
- Ask your child how he thinks a cow would sing the song. Making a cow sound, sing the song again using "moo" instead of the words.
- Continue to sing the song in other animal voices.
- Try to make your voice really sound like the animal. Rather than just saying the word "moo" as you sing, make the "moo" really sound like a cow.
- In addition to being a lot of fun, this game takes a lot of thinking on the part of your child.

High and Low   3+

DEVELOPS CONCEPT OF HIGH AND LOW

- Music sounds high and low. This is an important musical concept for young children to understand.
- Hold your hands high in the air and ask your child to copy you.
- Move your hands low to the ground and ask your child to copy you.
- Say the following poem, "High and low", with your child and do the appropriate actions.

> My hands go high. (hold hands high in the air)
> My hands go low. (hold hands low to the ground)
> Up high (hold hands high)
> Down low (hold hands low)
> This is how my hands go.

- Say this poem using different parts of the body—arms, feet, elbows and fingers.
- Reach your hands way up into the air "all the way to the sky." Then reach down "into the valley". Tell your child that when you make a high sound, she should imitate you and reach high into the sky. When you make a low sound, she should reach down low into the valley.

The I Can't Sing Book

The Volume Game   3+

This is a good game for teaching the concept of loud and soft.
An important benefit of this game is that your child will learn to talk
more softly when asked.

Choose a word that is fun to say and repeat the word over and over.
Start saying the word very softly and gradually say the word louder
and louder. You do it first and then let your child try to copy you.

Words that young children enjoy repeating include ice cream,
piccalilli, spaghetti, macaroni and teensy-weensy.

Start saying the word in a soft voice with your arms at your sides.
As your voice gets louder, gradually raise your arms up to the sky.

Say the word the loudest with your arms over your head and
gradually lower them as your voice gets softer.

Echoes   3+

Echoes are reflections of sounds that bounce back to you. In the
mountains, an echo bounces off the mountain and back again.

● Pretend to be a
mountain and tell your
child that when he says
a word, it will bounce
off you and back to
him.

Ask him to say the
word "hello" in a loud
voice.

You echo the sound
back to him.

Suggest that he say the
word "hello" in many
different ways—soft, fast,
slow, whisper, etc. Each
time you will echo the sound back to him.

Switch parts and let your child echo what you say.

Music Is...Sound

Sound or Silence 3+

● Distinguishing between sound and silence is an important concept in music. In music, the rests (silence) are just as important as the notes (sound). The following game and variations are an enjoyable way to teach this important skill.

● Play a recording on a cassette or CD player. While the music is playing, tiptoe around the room. When the music stops, stop moving and freeze in place.

● This game is a lot of fun because the players never know when the music will stop. Remember to emphasize that music means tiptoe and no music means freeze in place.

● A variation of this game is to sing or play a rhythm instrument while your child is moving.

● I have found that little children really enjoy the concept of "freeze". This is also a good word to use when you are trying to quieten down a noisy group.

Minute of Silence 3+

● Sit in a comfortable chair or sofa with your child. Tell him you are going to be quiet for one minute.

● Suggest that you both close your eyes as you listen to the sounds that you are hearing—inside noises, outside sounds and body sounds.

● When you talk about the sounds that you heard ask questions like:

Were the sounds loud or soft?
Were the sounds high or low?
Were the sounds far away or close?

● Games like this help young children appreciate quiet times and silence, a first step towards understanding the importance of rests (silence) in music.

Where's the Sound?

3+

- This game teaches auditory discrimination and positional language skills.
- Tell your child that you are going to another part of the room and that you will make a noise there.
- Ask him to hide his eyes and when he hears a noise (shake bells, bang drum, sing, clap hands, bang two forks together), to try and tell him where you are.

BANG BANG

- Encourage the use of words such as behind, close to, far away, up, down and on the side. Talk about these words before beginning this game.
- After you have played this a few times, ask your child to make the noises and you guess where he is.

Find the Music

3+

TEACHES SOUND AWARENESS

- Ask your child to hide his eyes while you place a musical toy somewhere in the room.
- Wind up the toy and then ask your child, "Where do you think the music is?"
- He can walk to the sound or tell you what he thinks.
- Take turns and let your child place the musical toy somewhere so you can guess where the music is.

Sound Signals   3+

● Pick two sounds. One sound could be clapping hands, the other coughing.
● Every time you clap your hands, it is time to sit down.
● Every time you cough, it is time to hop on one foot.
● This is great fun to do throughout the day.
● Use other sounds to signal things to do and your child will develop his listening skills at the same time.

Rain   3+

● Play rain music for your child or sing some rain songs like "It's raining, it's pouring" or "Incy Wincy Spider".
● Say the following poem and have your child repeat each line after you say it.

> Rain, rain—rain, rain
> Falling from the sky—falling from the sky
> Pitter, patter—pitter, patter
> Ooops, it hit my eye—oops, it hit my eye.
>
> Rain, rain—rain, rain
> Falling on my toys—falling on my toys
> Boom, boom, boom, boom—boom, boom, boom, boom
> Scary sounding noise—scary sounding noise.
>
> Rain, rain—rain, rain
> Falling on my nose—falling on my nose
> Drip, drip, drip, drip—drip, drip, drip, drip
> Squishing through my toes—squishing through my toes.
>   Jackie Silberg

The I Can't Sing Book

● Play the "Rain Game", making rain sounds.

> Pitter patter—tap your hands gently on your knees
> Rain getting louder—hit your knees harder and faster
> Thunder—keep your hands moving and add your stamping feet
> Lightning—slap your hands together to make a cracking sound

● Now say the chant again.

Feel the Vibes   3+

● Sound is produced by the movement of air. This movement of the air is called vibration.
● Here are some ways to experience vibration.

> ✔ Touch your hand to your throat. Now, hum. Can you feel your throat vibrating?
> ✔ Hold the palm of one hand about an inch in front of your mouth. Now, blow on your hand. You will hear a faint but distinct sound. Hold up the index finger of the other hand and move it through the air flow.
> ✔ Can you hear the sound changing?

Music Is...Sound

✔ Cut a rubber band so that it lies in one straight, flat piece. Two people hold the ends of the rubber band and stretch it out until it is fairly taut. A third person plucks the rubber band in the middle to produce a sound. Pull the rubber band tighter. The tighter that you pull, the higher the sound. Be careful not to pull the rubber band too tight or it might snap and hurt someone. Notice that the looser the rubber band is, the lower the sound.

● Look for other things that vibrate. Many appliances are good examples—air conditioners, hair dryers, refrigerators and furnaces.
● Say the following poem:

> Vibration makes the air move,
> And that's what makes the sound.
> So listen, listen, listen,
> There's sound all around.
>
> Jackie Silberg

Sound Fun

TEACHES SOUND AWARENESS

● Play recorded music. Let your child move to the rhythm of the music. You can also clap your hands, click your tongue and stamp your feet.
● Draw the rhythm of a song on paper. Slow rhythms may be soft and wavy lines; fast rhythms may be dark and heavier lines. Hold your child's hand and guide it to the music. What kind of lines would you draw if you were listening to marching music?
● Show your child how to make a clicking sound with his mouth. Sing a song and let your child accompany you with his clicks. The clicks sound very much like a maraca (a gourd filled with seeds).
● Sing part of a song loudly and part softly. "Yankee doodle" and "Jingle bells" are both excellent for singing loud and soft. Do the first part loudly and the second part softly, or reverse the two.
● Make a sound with your body. Stamp your feet, snap your fingers or click your tongue. Let your child hide his eyes and guess what sound you are making.

The I Can't Sing Book

What's That Sound? 4+

TEACHES AUDITORY DISCRIMINATION

- You will need two or three others to play this game.
- Two children stand with their backs to you.
- Each child is asked to think of an animal sound that they can make.
- With their backs towards you, they begin to make the animal sounds at the same time.
- The other children tell what animal sounds they hear.
- This game takes a lot of concentration and children really enjoy it.
- Try this with transportation sounds—cars, aeroplanes, fire engines, trains, motorcycles.

Listen for the Sound 4+

DEVELOPS LISTENING SKILLS

- This is an excellent game for a birthday party.
- Play a short piece of music for a group of children.
- Talk about several things to listen for. Ask each child to pick one thing to listen for.
- Things to listen for are soft sounds, fast sounds, high sounds, low sounds and happy sounds.
- Play the music and when it is over, ask the children what kind of sounds they heard.
- As each child tells what kind of sound he heard, ask the group if someone else would like to choose that sound for next time.
- Continue exchanging the sounds and then play the music again.
- The more the children listen for different sounds, the better their auditory skills will be.

Animal sounds are easy to make, and, since little children are learning to talk, it's a lot easier to make one or two sounds instead of an entire sentence. The sounds are also fun and very musical.

Hose Singing

4+

● You will need a soft hose long enough to put one end at your mouth and the other at your ear.

● Demonstrate how to sing into the hose and listen to your voice with your ear.

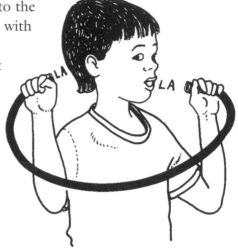

● Give it to your child and put one end at his mouth and the other end at his ear.

● First you sing (softly) into the hose. Ask him what he hears.

● Now let him sing into the hose. Does he recognize his voice?

More High and Low

4+

● Young children have difficulty with the concept of high and low sounds in music. They often confuse it with loud and soft.

● Here are some games to help establish the concept of high and low.

● Take a fluttery object like a scarf and watch it float to the ground. It starts high and falls low to the ground. Try moving like the scarf as you gently float to the ground.

● Take two water glasses, a large and a small one. Tap gently on each glass. Help your child differentiate between the two sounds.

The I Can't Sing Book

- Sing the major scale from low to high—doh, ray, me, fah, soh, lah, te, doh. Begin with your hands on your toes and, as you sing the scale upward, gradually raise your hands high into the air. Then, sing the scale downward and gradually move your fingers downward until they are back on your toes.

Different Voices

DEVELOPS LISTENING SKILLS

- Did you ever think about the many ways that you can make your voice sound? Changing the quality of your voice and the rhythm of your words are excellent experiences in sound awareness.
- Pick a word or phrase that is fun to say. "Ice cream" is a favourite.
- Here are different ways to say the word.

> hold your nose
> cup your hands around your mouth
> loud and soft
> fast and slow
> pucker your lips
> put your hand over your mouth

- Practise saying the word "ice cream" different ways. Then, pick a different word and say it different ways.
- If your child enjoys this game, try saying short sentences in different ways too.

Nature Instruments

TEACHES CREATIVITY

- Go for a nature walk and try to make an instrument from objects found on the way.
- A branch with rubber bands stretched across it makes a nice harp.
- Blowing through two blades of grass held between the thumbs creates a vibrating sound like a whistle.

Music Is...Sound

The Paper Game 4+

● Many sounds can be made with paper. You can crunch it, tear it, shake it, cut it, fan with it and run your fingers on it while it is held in the air. (This is also a great way to re-use paper.)

● Pick a familiar song like the "The farmer's in his den" and at the end of each line make a paper sound.

> The farmer's in his den. (crunch paper)
> The farmer's in his den. (crunch paper)
> Hi, ho, the derry-o, (crunch paper)
> The farmer's in his den. (crunch paper)

● Sing it again and make a different paper sound at the end of each line.

● Another game you can play is to pick two paper sounds, for example, crunch and tear. Do these sounds several times so that your child becomes familiar with the sound.

● Let your child hide his eyes while you make one of the paper sounds. Then ask your child which sound you made.

Making Music in the Kitchen 4+

● Play a game with kitchen utensils. Put an egg beater, flour sifter, spoons, pots and pans on a table.

● Pick up each utensil one at a time and make a sound with it. Turn the egg beater, hit a spoon on a pot, etc. Let your child do this too.

● Say the following poem and make a sound with one of the utensils. Ask your child if she can tell you which utensil you are using.

> I'm making music with something in the kitchen.
> Can you guess what it is?
> I'm making music with something in the kitchen.
> One, two, three...guess!

● Try having a kitchen band. Sing a song with your child and accompany your singing with the kitchen instruments.

The I Can't Sing Book

I Hear a Word   4+

In this music game children listen for words in a poem or song.

Select a special word. With young children, choose a word that occurs often in the poem or song. With older children it can occur less frequently, or they can select the word.

Tell your child the special word and instruct him to wave his hands in the air when he hears the special word.

For example, if the poem is "Humpty Dumpty", he can wave his hands in the air each time he hears the words "Humpty Dumpty".

Pick a song or a poem in which the same word appears more than one time. Some suggestions are "Pat-a-cake", "This little pig went to market", and "Mary had a little lamb".

Think of other ways to signal hearing the word—jump up and down, wiggle your fingers, shake your head.

● A variation of this game is to listen for words that begin with the same sound. This is especially good for five and six year olds.

Listening in Rhythm   4+

This game uses rhythm to teach sequence and recall. Tell your child that you are going to say a sentence and make sounds with your body too.

Say the following:

> My name is Sally and I can cough, cough, cough.
> (cough instead of saying the word)

Ask your child to copy you and say the same sentence putting in his name.

Now add another body sound to your sentence.

> My name is Sally and I can cough, cough, cough and jump,
> jump, jump. (cough and jump instead of saying the words)

- Keep adding more body sounds depending on the age of your child. A five year old can usually do six or seven.
- Other body sounds and movements you can try include:

  wiggle your tongue
  sniff with your nose
  snap your fingers
  whistle
  clap your hands
  stamp your feet
  wave your arms

Cheek Popping

TEACHES COORDINATION AND COUNTING SKILLS

- Fill your cheeks full of air. Keep your mouth closed. When your cheeks are completely full, take the palms of your hands and pop your cheeks.
- Try singing the song "Jingle bells" but instead of singing the words "jingle bells" pop your cheeks three times and sing the rest of the words.

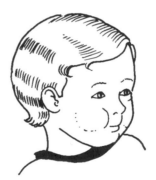

The I Can't Sing Book

Harder Cheek Popping

TEACHES LISTENING SKILLS

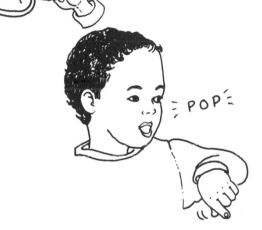

- Put your index finger into your mouth. Place it along the side of your cheek and hold it lightly with your lips. Pop your finger out of the corner of your mouth and you will hear a popping sound.
- Say the following poem and pop your cheek each time you hear the word "pop."

> Popcorn, popcorn,
> Pop, pop, pop
> Popcorn, popcorn,
> Pop, pop, pop
> Fluffy and white,
> Fun to bite
> Popcorn, popcorn,
> Pop, pop, pop.

♪ **While waiting in the queue at a checkout counter, the father in front of me was playing with his young child. "What does the horsey say?" the father asked. The child gave a whinny. "What does the cow say?" the father asked. "Moo," replied the child. Sound familiar? Have you ever wondered why young children are so fascinated with animals and insects and why they love to make the sounds of cows, dogs, bees and especially pigs?**

Music Is...Sound

Music is inborn says Dr Mark Tramo, a neurobiologist at Harvard Medical School. Babies hear and distinguish sounds before birth. Numerous studies indicate that a newborn can identify his mother's voice from other voices around him, and that at birth he already has a preference for the kind of music his mother listened to in pregnancy.

chapter 4

Music Is...
Language

For the past 19 years I have been teaching music classes with parents and children together. There is a remarkable improvement in language development after two weeks of this class. How do I know? The parents tell me. Even infants recognize words, sounds, rhythms, tones and pitches long before they talk, sing or dance. Music teaches the rhythm of language. When you sing, you put vowels and consonants in a rhythmic pattern that enhances language skills. So the more music your child has in her life, the more likely she will develop good speaking and reading skills.

Activities and Games That Explore Language

Where Is Thumbkin? $1\frac{1}{2}^+$

- The popular song "Where Is Thumbkin" is a great favourite of little children.
- A very creative way to sing this song is to use a different voice for each finger. For example:

> Where is Thumbkin? Where is Thumbkin?
> Here I am, here I am. (sing this in a different kind of voice—happy, grumpy, sad, funny or whiny)
> How are you this morning? (regular voice)
> Very well, I thank you. (different voice)
> Run away, run away. (regular voice)

The Announcement Song 2^+

- Teach your child how to sing announcements.
- Instead of saying, "It's time for breakfast", why not sing it?
- Think of all the announcements that you can make all day long with song.

> Time to put shoes on
> Lunch time
> It's time to go outside
> Grandma is coming today
>
> and lots more....

Incy Wincy Spider

2

DEVELOPS LANGUAGE SKILLS

● This game teaches many skills: listening, language acquisition and how to pay attention. First learn the song and then add the actions.

> The incy wincy spider went up the water spout.
>   (move fingers up to the sky like a spider)
> Down came the rain and washed the spider out.
>   (move fingers down from the sky like rain)
> Out came the sun and dried up all the rain.
>   (make a big circle with hands for the sun)
> And the incy wincy spider went up the spout again.
>   (move fingers up to the sky like a spider)

incy wincy

spider went ...

● After learning the song, sing it many times in many different ways. The actions are the same, however, no matter how many different ways you sing it. Other ways to sing the song include:

> La, la, la
> Hum
> Whistle
> Beginning letter sounds—ga, ga; da, da; ta, ta, ta or the beginning sound of your name or your child's name.
> No singing, only the actions—you'll be amazed at how quiet the children are!

Give Me an "S"   2+

- Try spelling familiar words or names with this familiar sports chant.
- Start with your child's name. Say each letter and clap two times.

> Give me an "S" (clap...clap)
> Give me an "A" (clap...clap)
> Give me an "M" (clap...clap)

- Say the word and yell "yea" as you jump up and down.

Chanting Games   2+

- Chanting is an important part of the musical development of a young child. The organization of words is enhanced and a feeling for rhythm and rhyme is developed.
- Young children love repetition in words, in sounds and in syllables.
- Choose a poem that has a definite rhythm and is appealing to a young child. "Miss Mary Mack", an old Americn skipping rope chant, is one that young children enjoy.

> Miss Mary Mack, Mack, Mack
> All dressed in black, black, black
> With silver buttons, buttons, buttons
> Up and down her back, back, back.
> She asked her mother, mother, mother
> For fifteen pence, pence, pence
> To see the elephants, elephants, elephants
> Jump the fence, fence, fence.
> They jumped so high, high, high
> They reached the sky, sky, sky
> And they didn't come back, back, back
> Till the fourth of July, ly, ly.

- Add body sounds, such as clapping and snapping or rhythm instruments such as drums and rhythm sticks to add another dimension to the chant.
- Make up your own chants. Use the ones you know as guides.

> Miss Betty Blue, Blue, Blue
> Learned to say moo, moo, moo, etc.

Make a Chant

2+

- Pick out something that your child loves to do such as building a tower with blocks or painting a picture.
- Make up a chant about one of her favourite things.

> Drawing a picture, red and blue
> Drawing a picture, and yellow, too.

- Say the chant three times. First in a regular voice, second in a very loud voice and third in a very soft voice.
- You can change the tone of your voice—high, low, sad, happy, grumpy, etc.

Magic Word

2+

DEVELOPS LISTENING SKILLS

- Pick a favourite song to sing.
- Tell your child that whenever she hears a certain word she should clap her hands.
- For example, with "Old MacDonald Had a Farm", each time you hear the word "farm", clap your hands.
- Other actions you can do each time you hear the word "farm" are sit down, stamp your feet, change seats or jump up and down.

Music Is...Language

Sequencing Songs

DEVELOPS COGNITIVE SKILLS

- Sometimes called "add on" songs, sequencing songs prepare children for reading and other academic skills.
- Maths uses sequencing, history employs sequencing and memory is developed with sequencing.
- Songs that have certain parts that keep repeating or that always go back to the beginning for the repeat are sequencing songs.

I Know an Old Lady Who
Swallowed a Fly
The Twelve Days of Christmas
Old MacDonald Had a Farm
The Farmer in the Dell
I Had a Rooster
She'll Be Comin' 'Round the
Mountain

- Can you add to this list?

Research has shown that preschool children enrolled in music programmes experience tremendous boosts in spatial IQ scores as compared to children with no music training.

The I Can't Sing Book

Poetry in Rhythm   3+

- Select a favourite poem or nursery rhyme. I have chosen "Peas Porridge Hot" for this example.
- Ask your child to "echo" what you say.

> Adult—Peas porridge hot
> Child—Peas porridge hot
> Adult—Peas porridge cold
> Child—Peas porridge cold
> Adult—Peas porridge in the pot
> Child—Peas porridge in the pot
> Adult—Nine days old
> Child—Nine days old

- Now say two lines, "Peas porridge hot, peas porridge cold."
- Let your child say the next two lines, "Peas porridge in the pot, nine days old." Continue with:

> Some like it hot,
> Some like it cold,
> Some like it in the pot
> Nine days old.

- Speaking rhythmically is a wonderful pre-reading skill.

What's the Word?   3+

- Pick a song that your child likes. Sing the song several times to be sure that she knows the words.
- Sing the song and begin to leave out words. Start by leaving out the last word of each line.
- As your child begins to understand and enjoy this game, take turns singing the song and stopping at any point for the other person to continue the song.

Singing Telephones

DEVELOPS LISTENING SKILLS

- Have a telephone conversation with your child on two toy telephones.
- Sing one line of a familiar song and ask her to sing it back to you.
- Make up melodies to go with questions like, "How are you?" or "What did you have for lunch?" Encourage your child to sing the answers back to you.
- Singing about your day is similar to an opera. Make the songs as dramatic as you wish!

Make a Face

4+

DEVELOPS AN AWARENESS OF FEELINGS

- Talk about different kinds of feelings. Each time you talk about the feeling, the child makes a face to express that feeling. Happy, angry, scared and sad are good ones to start with.
- Choose a favourite song and as you sing it, make your face and your voice express a particular feeling. For example, sing the song smiling and in a happy voice. Some other ways to sing are:

    In a low voice with an angry face
    In a crying voice with a sad face
    With a soft voice and a scared face.

The I Can't Sing Book

Operetta Fun   4+

DEVELOPS LANGUAGE AND IMAGINATION

● Sing about something that you do. Instead of telling a story with words only, add music to the words.
● A good subject for your operetta is "Building a Tower".
● Here's an idea of what the dialogue might be; just make up your own tune.

> Here are big and little blocks. Put one on the bottom and then add another, and so on.

● Other ideas: going to the park, what is in the supermarket and playing with toys.

Lyrical Fun   4+

DEVELOPS COGNITIVE THINKING

● Did you ever experience really hearing the words to a song for the first time although you had been singing it for a long time?
● We all sing songs but sometimes don't think about what the words mean.
● It's fun to discuss the words to songs with your child.
● For example, "Twinkle, Twinkle, Little Star". Ask your child questions like, "What do you think 'how I wonder what you are' means?" You will be amazed at the answers you will get. This kind of game helps children to think about the things that they hear more carefully.
● It's good to talk about the lyrics of all of the songs that your child enjoys singing. It will also make singing the song more meaningful.

**Music teaches young children ...
to achieve happiness through self-expression, to respect performance skills in other people, to appreciate many cultures and to develop a foundation for further musical studies.**

Are You Sleeping?

● Here are the words to "Are You Sleeping" in other languages. This is the same tune as "Frère Jacques" and "Where Is Thumbkin?"

Are you sleeping, are you sleeping
Brother John, brother John?
Morning bells are ringing, morning bells are ringing
Ding, ding, dong. Ding, ding, dong.

Spanish

Fray Felipe, Fray Felipe,
(Fry feh lee pay, fry feh lee pay)
Duermes tu? Duermes tu?
(D'wear mess too, d'wear mess too)
Toca la campana, Toca la campana
(Toe kah la com pa nah, Toe kah la com pa nah)
Bam, bam, bam. Bam, bam, bam.

French

Frère Jacques, frère Jacques
(Frair uh jhak uh, Frair uh jhak uh)
Dormez vous? Dormez vous?
(Door may voo, door may voo)
Sonnez les matines. Sonnez les matines.
(sun ay lay ma teen uh, sun ay lay ma teen uh)
Dan, dan don. Dan, dan, don.

German

Bruder Jakob, Bruder Jakob
    (Broo der Ya kobe (long o), Broo der Ya kobe)
Schlafst du noch? Schlafst du noch?
    (Shlafst do nak, Shlafst do nak)
Morgenglocken lauten. Morgenglocken lauten.
    (Morgan glocken loyten, Morgan glocken loyten)
Bim, bam, bim. Bim, bam, bim.

Language Can Be Silly, Too

My granddaughter's current joke at age 3 $\frac{1}{2}$ years is "Mummy's got dirt in her hair." This is followed by endless laughter. Don't you just love to see children laugh and giggle? It's so fascinating to see what is amusing to a young child.

Nonsense words (bibbity boppity boo) and taking familiar situations and changing them (my doggie had dinner at the table) are two ideas that make little children laugh. What kind of silly song do children most enjoy? I think a song that doesn't make sense or a silly story like "On Top of Spaghetti", or nonsense like "Do Your Ears Hang Low?" are good examples. Songs about crazy characters, syncopated songs, nonsense rhymes, tongue twisters, riddles and jokes and songs that won't end are all silly to young children.

There is an underlying value in singing silly songs. We all have many complex and confusing things to deal with in our lives and singing silly songs helps us relax, enjoy the humour and release tension. For young children, these songs also teach language development and encourage their sense of humour.

Some of my favourite silly songs are:

The Old Lady Who Swallowed a Fly
Down By the Bay
On Top of Spaghetti
Boom, Boom Ain't It Great to Be Crazy
Miss Mary Mack
Peas Porridge Hot
Peanut Butter
The Ants Go Marching
Baby Bumble Bee
Clementine
Five Little Monkeys
Michael Finnegan
Do Your Ears Hang Low?
I'm Being Swallowed by a Boa Constrictor

The I Can't Sing Book

chapter 5

• Music Is...

Movement

Did you ever see a young child sit still for more than a couple of minutes? Moving is a fundamental activity for young children. They jump, they hop, they tumble...they are in constant motion. Through movement children learn gross and fine motor skills, a sense of rhythm and spatial awareness. Music and movement are intertwined. Movement expresses the rhythm of music with your body. The movement can be smooth or bumpy, fast or slow, loud or soft. When young children hear music they automatically begin to bounce and rock. Eventually this rocking and bouncing will develop into a steady rhythm or beat that follows the music. This steady rhythm or beat will help in developing language and motor skills and cognitive thinking. All of the games and activities in this chapter can be done with music playing in the background or without music.

Activities and Games That Explore Movement

Hello, Body 1+

TEACHES RHYTHM EXPRESSION WITH BODY MOVEMENT

AND TEACHES ABOUT PARTS OF THE BODY

● Say this poem and do the actions. Encourage your child to do it with you.

Hello, feet
Let's feel the beat. (tap foot on the floor)

Hello, knees
Zip a dee dee. (bend knees)

Hello, thigh
My, oh, my. (move leg back and forth at the thigh)

Hello, hip
Pip, pip, pip. (roll hips around and around)

Hello, shoulder
Get a little older. (move shoulders in a circular motion)

Hello, neck
Picky, picky, peck. (stretch neck)

Hello, head
Go to bed. (move head towards shoulder, close eyes and pretend to sleep.)

Jackie Silberg

● You can also pretend to snore on the last line.

The I Can't Sing Book

Moving and Stopping $1\frac{1}{2}$+

DEVELOPS LISTENING SKILLS

Choose an instrumental recording that has soft gentle music.
Start out with tiptoe steps to the music.
Tell your child that when the music stops, he will freeze in place.
Start the music again and this time take larger steps.
Stop the music again.
Each time you stop the music, you or your child can suggest a new way to move when the music starts again.

I'm a Walking $1\frac{1}{2}$+

DEVELOPS MOTOR SKILL

These activities will surely become some of your child's favourites.
You can use them at any time of the day.
Hold your child's hand and sing or say the following poem, "I'm a Walking".

> I'm a walking, walking, walking
> I'm a walking, walking, walking
> I'm a walking, walking, walking
> Then I stop!
> > Jackie Silberg

Walk around the room and on the word "stop" freeze in place.
Try skipping, hopping, jumping, skating, swimming, running, tiptoeing and marching.
● Ask your child for suggestions of other things to do with this song. He will probably have lots of wonderful ideas.

Jumping Jacks

2+

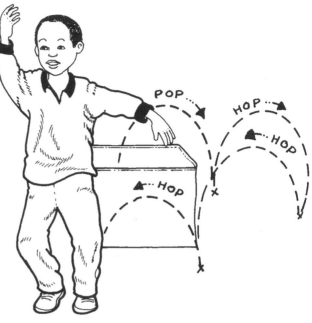

- Pretend to be a jumping jack in a box. Stoop down low and be very quiet.
- When the music starts, pop out of your box and jump around the room.
- When the music stops, jump back into your box.
- Young children really enjoy this game.

Let's Dance 2+

TEACHES ABOUT PARTS OF THE BODY

- Play some fast music that your child enjoys.
- Sit or stand to play the game.
- Tell your child to "dance your feet". Show him how to move his feet.
- Now "dance your arms". Show him how to move his arms.
- Try dancing your knees, elbows, legs, hands, fingers, head, shoulders and your entire body.

Waltzing

2+

DEVELOPS CREATIVE MOVEMENT

- Play waltz music for your child.
- Hold his hand or hold him in your arms and dance around the room to the music.
- Let him take his favourite stuffed animal and dance with it, swirling and twirling.

The I Can't Sing Book

My Toes Are Starting to Wiggle 2+

TEACHES THE NAMES OF PARTS OF THE BODY

Sing the song and do the movements that the song suggests.

Sing to the tune of "For He's a Jolly Good Fellow".

My toes are starting to wiggle,
My toes are starting to wiggle,
My toes are starting to wiggle,
Around and around and around.

More verses are:

My hands are starting to clap...
My feet are starting to stomp...
My eyes are starting to blink...
My fingers are starting to scratch...
My ears are starting to listen...

Hickory Dickory Dock 2+

TEACHES RHYTHM AND EYE-HAND COORDINATION

Face your child. One of you is the clock and the other is the mouse.

The clock stands stiffly and puts his arms straight out in front of him.

Say or sing the song as you do the following actions.

Hickory, Dickory, Dock,
The mouse ran up the clock. (the mouse runs up the clock's arms
    with his fingers)
The clock struck one. (the clock holds up one finger)
The mouse ran down. (the mouse runs down the clock's arms with
    his fingers)
Hickory, Dickory, Dock.

Music Is...Movement

All Aboard

● Say the following words as you turn the wheels of the train with your arms.

> Get on board, everybody.
> Get on board, everybody.
> Get on board, everybody.
> The music train is here.
>
> We're chugging down the track, everybody.
> We're chugging down the track, everybody.
> We're chugging down the track, everybody.
> The music train is here. (walk around the room as you
> turn the wheels of the train)
>
> Let's stop right here for a song, everybody.
> Let's stop right here for a song, everybody.
> Let's stop right here for a song, everybody.
> The music train is here.

● Pick a song and everybody sing it together.
● Start the song again, say the three verses and then sing another song.

The I Can't Sing Book

Sound Off
3+

Here are ways to make sounds:

Singing	Talking
Humming	Whistling
Breathing	Laughing
Hissing	Sighing
Sneezing	Coughing
Clapping	Clicking
Crying	Knocking
Slapping	Stamping
Tapping	Playing an instrument

This game asks you to make your body move the way the sound feels. Laughing and singing would indicate that you feel happy and you can move accordingly.

Crying means you are sad, and you move as if you were sad.

Coughing and sneezing means you are ill and you move as if you are ill.

● You can play music to set the mood. Play happy music, sad music and scary music.

Some moving ideas are crawling, skipping with a smile, walking slowly, tiptoeing, elephant walking, etc.

Body Part Dancing
3+

Cut holes in a large box.

Let your child get in the box and put his hands or feet or head through the holes.

Play music and your child moves to the music using the body part that is sticking out of the box.

Switch parts. This is as much fun to watch as it is to do.

The Human Machine 3+

DEVELOPS COORDINATION AND LISTENING SKILLS

- Sit or stand to play this game.
- Choose a body part and keep it in constant motion. For example, move one knee up and down or one arm back and forth.
- Play music as you are doing this movement. Pick music that goes fast and slow and tell the "machine" (child) to listen to the music and go faster or slower when the music goes faster or slower.

Mirror/Shadow 3+

DEVELOPS OBSERVATION SKILLS

Mirror

- Children will need partners to play this game.
- The partners face each other and pretend to be looking into a mirror.
- The "mirror" imitates all of the actions of the other person. If the person looking into the "mirror" jumps up and down, the "mirror" jumps up and down; if the person looking into the "mirror" turns around, the "mirror" turns around, etc.
- Other movement ideas are to shake hands, nod heads, wave arms and make faces.

Shadow

- This game is the counterpart to "Mirror".
- It is played the same way, except that the "shadow" follows the partner as he moves around the room hopping, skipping and jumping.
- Play music with both the "Mirror" and "Shadow" games. Let the music guide the movements.

The I Can't Sing Book

Movement in the Wind   3+

TEACHES AWARENESS OF RHYTHMS IN NATURE

- Talk about the wind. What is the wind? What makes the wind? What causes the wind to change directions?
- What can the wind blow? Leaves, kites, balloons, litter? Does a leaf blow slowly, fast, up and down? Does the wind blow snowflakes and rain?
- Pretend to be:

> a leaf fluttering to the ground slowly
> a leaf blowing across the garden quickly
> a hailstone falling to the ground
> a raindrop falling to the earth
> a feather blown by the wind
> a snowflake blown by the wind

- The wind feels different in the summer than in the winter. It also feels different if you are riding in a car with the window open.

Tap Dancing   3+

DEVELOPS MOTOR SKILLS AND IMAGINATION

- Don't you just love to watch tap dancing? Well, you can do it too.
- Make your own tap shoes. All you do is glue coins on the soles and heels of comfortable shoes. Larger coins work best. When the glue dries you are ready to dance the night away.
- Put on music that your child likes and move your dancing feet.
- Here are some tap steps to do that are easy and that will make the best sounds.

> ✓ Start with slow walking on the floor. Each time you step your foot down you will hear a sound.
> ✓ Marching gives your tapping a wonderful sound.
> ✓ Shuffling is a popular tap step. Stand on one foot and with the other foot you brush your foot back and forth. If you want to become professional, do a "shuffle step". You brush forward, brush backward and step down. There are three actions and if you say the words "shuffle step" you will master it easily.

Exploring Space 4+

- Play soft, slow music for relaxing.
- Sit on the floor and reach out your hands to explore all the space around you—in front, behind, next to, above and underneath. Now do the same with your legs.
- Stand with your feet a shoulder's width apart. Let your arms hang limp, like a rag doll. Slowly bend over at the waist until your fingertips touch the floor. Try to remain in this position for a few seconds. Relax totally. Slowly straighten up, feeling each body part straightening one at a time; first the hips, then the waist, back and shoulders and finally the head.

Magnets 4+

- Sit on the floor and pretend that one of your hands is a magnet and the rest of your body can be magnetized.
- What happens when you bring the magnet (your hand) to your knee, your foot, your head or your stomach?
- Try to move around while the magnet (your hand) is attached to another part of your body.

The I Can't Sing Book

Follow the Leader

4+

- This game should be played with several children. It's an excellent birthday party game.
- Everyone sits in a circle and the leader chooses a movement for everyone to copy. It's best to start this game with an adult leader.
- While the leader is doing the movement—tapping the floor, tapping knees, clapping hands—the others will watch carefully and copy the leader.
- As the leader changes from one movement to another, the others change with the leader.
- Variations of this game include:

  ✓ Everyone stands in a circle and the leader does movements with his feet only.
  ✓ While standing, the leader uses all parts of the body— swinging arms, shaking hips, moving head back and forth and wiggling fingers.

- Another variation is for one child to leave the room. When he returns, the rest of the group is following the movements of a secret leader. The child has to guess who the leader is. Everyone gets a turn at leaving the room and coming back to guess the leader. Children really love to do this!

Speaking With Your Body

4+

DEVELOPS BODY CONTROL AND IMAGINATION

- Children can be very expressive with their bodies. This exercise is good to loosen up the body and is also a lot of fun.
- Tell your child that you are going to speak with your body. How do you say "yes" with your body? You move your head up and down. How do you say "no" with your body? You move your head back and forth.
- Practise saying "yes" and "no" with your head.

Music Is...Movement

● All the parts of your body can say "yes" and "no". Say "yes" with your head, arms, shoulders and elbows. Say "no" with the same body parts.

● Say "yes" with your hips, legs, ankles and toes. Now, repeat and say "no".

● Make up questions that can be answered "yes" or "no". For example, "Do you like pizza?"

● Try having part of the day when everything will be answered with a part of the body, not words. Remember that your child gets to ask you questions also that can only be answered with parts of your body.

● Think of different parts of the body and what kind of movement would express language. Here are ideas to get you started.

Part of the body	What it says
Nose	I smell something yummy
Nose	I smell something yucky
Eyes	I'm happy
Eyes	I'm sad
Head	Yes
Head	No
Shoulders	I don't know
Hands	Stop
Foot	I'm waiting
Elbow	Move out of the way
Neck	I can't see
Hands	I like you

● Try to have a conversation with movement only.

The I Can't Sing Book

Children relate to animal movement because it is similar to their own. Whenever you want to teach a concept, think about how you can incorporate animals into the idea that you want to teach. What parent or teacher hasn't asked a child to be "quiet as a mouse?"

Clap Together   5+

DEVELOPS EYE-HAND COORDINATION

● Five year olds love to play this game.
● Here is the clapping game.

> Both clap your hands on your thighs two times.
> Clap your hands together two times.
> Clap each other's hands two times (palms straight up).
> Clap your own hands two times.

● Try the clapping game while singing a familiar song.

Jean Piaget's research showed that "the more a child sees and hears, the more he wants to see and hear." Researchers have discovered that Piaget's theory holds true in the area of music. Edwin E. Gordon, a music researcher, believes that what is absorbed unconsciously before the age of three directly affects the language development in later years. He calls this process "unconscious listening".

chapter 6

Music Is...

Singing

Even if you do not think of yourself as a singer, try to remember all the songs that you know how to sing (yes, "Happy Birthday" and "The ABC Song" count). Do you have a favourite song? Do you remember where you learned your favourite song? Chances are you learned a song because you heard it sung, played on the radio, television or even on a record or CD, or it reminds you of a happy or important time. Right now, make a list of 10 songs that you can sing. Pick one of those songs and teach it to your child. It doesn't have to be a children's song; it can be any song that you enjoy singing.

4 Ideas...
for Learning a Song

1. Think about the song that you want to teach. Why do you like it? Do you like the words? The melody? The rhythm? Knowing what you like about a song will help you learn it faster and when you teach it, your child will pick up on your interest and enthusiasm.

2. Sing the song again and again in different ways until you have learned it completely. Sing it slowly, sing it softly, sing it loud, etc. Learning a song can be very simple.

3. Learn the words first, then add the melody. Sing it over and over until you are confident. Young children will never criticize your voice, but they will surely know if you are unsure of yourself.

4. When learning a new song, try practising it in front of a mirror. If possible, have non-judgmental family members or friends be your audience.

10 Ideas...
for Teaching a Song

Repetition

1. Sing the song two or three times. Then, sing the song again and leave out a key word. Ask your child to fill in the blank. For example: "Twinkle, twinkle, little _____".

Say It First

2. Try speaking the words first and ask your child to say them back to you. When she has learned the words, then you can add the melody.

Call and Response

3. Another tried-and-true method for teaching a song is "call and response". This means that you sing one line of a song and ask your child to sing it back to you. For example, sing "For He's a Jolly Good Fellow" and then ask your child to sing the same phrase.

Clap Out the Rhythm

4. Use the rhythm of the song to teach it to your child. Clap out the rhythm first and ask your child to clap with you. Then, say the words with the rhythm. Example:

Twin-kle Twin-kle Lit-tle Star
/   /   /   /   /   /   /

(Each / is a clap.)

What's the Story?

5. Talk about the words of the song. What does the song mean? For instance, in the song "Yankee Doodle", focus on the action. What is happening? Where did Yankee Doodle go? How did he go to town? What did he do once he arrived? Encourage children to think about the words (and act them out); this will help them to remember the song. Songs that are good for acting out:

Peas Porridge Hot
Five Little Monkeys
Row, Row, Row Your Boat
Hickory Dickory Dock
Incy Wincy Spider
Pop Goes the Weasel
Old MacDonald Had a Farm

Music Is...Singing

Pictures Tell a Story

6. Use pictures to reinforce the words. For example, when teaching the song "The Wheels on the Bus" use pictures of a wheel, a bus, windscreen wipers and a baby crying. Cut out pictures from magazines that match the words to the song or search for pictures in magazines or books. For example, look for pictures of the animals on the farm to go with "Old MacDonald Had a Farm".

Use Flannel Boards

7. Another way to teach a song is to use a flannel board (to make your own, cover a board with felt or flannel). For example, in the song "The Old Lady Who Swallowed a Fly" you can make felt patterns of the different animals in the song. The fly, bird, cat, dog, cow and horse. Each time you sing the name of the animal, put the pattern on the flannel board.

Children Love Puppets

8. For a variation on the call and response method, use puppets to be the leaders. For example, teach "Mary Had a Little Lamb" using a puppet that looks like a lamb.

Big Voices and Little Voices

9. Sing the song in a loud or soft voice, depending on which is appropriate to the song. For example, sing a lullaby in a soft voice and a marching type song in a big voice. Or, try using a different sounding voice to reinforce the meaning of the song. For example, you could teach a Halloween song in a low, spooky voice. Teach the song "The Incy Wincy Spider" in a high, soft voice.

Use a Tape Recorder

10. Play a tape of the song that you want to teach; play it again and sing along with it. This technique leaves your hands free to use

The I Can't Sing Book

gestures, to move as you sing and to employ visual reinforcements. Above all, teach songs that you enjoy—the children will like them too.

If you enjoy music and sing with enthusiasm, children will respond. Children are interested in the words, the song and the actions. They love to participate and sing the same song over and over just for the joy of singing. Following are some ways to evaluate whether children are enjoying the music that you play or sing for them.

If they join in the singing
How long their attention span is when listening
What songs the children ask to hear
Comments that the children make about the music
Changes that the children make to the music
If you hear them singing or humming the song later
in the day or week

Some songs have the same melody. For example, if you can sing "Twinkle, Twinkle, Little Star" you can also sing "Baa, Baa Black Sheep" and "The ABC Song". If you can sing "Frère Jacques" or the English version "Are You Sleeping?" you can also sing "Where Is Thumbkin?"

Some popular songs have used classical music as the melody. "I'm Always Chasing Rainbows" is from "The Fantasie Impromptu" by Chopin. The song "Till the End of Time" is also a melody by Chopin. Singing is a joyous experience for everyone—teachers, parents and children. Good luck and good singing!

Songs to Sing... British Style

Folk songs are songs written from the heart. The songs come from people's experiences and have lyrics that are easy to sing. Folk songs are excellent to sing with young children because they are repetitive and have an easy-to-sing vocal range and a simple melody.

Every nation in the world sings. Every country, including the Great Britain, has some form of song handed down in the oral tradition from one generation to the next. These songs cover a wide variety of styles and subjects, from all parts of the United Kingdom.

Following is a list of songs that are part of our country's folklore. You may already know one stanza of the song and the melody, which makes it easy to teach. Pick out your favourites!

Patriotic Songs

God Save the Queen

Jerusalem

The Blue Bells of Scotland

Rule, Britannia

Danny Boy

March of the Men of Harlech

Ballads

Cockles and Mussels

The Bonny, Bonny Banks of Loch Lomond

Comin' Through the Rye

My Bonny Lies Over the Ocean

Oh Where, Oh Where Has My Little Dog Gone?

Folk/Traditional Songs

Are You Sleeping?

The Hokey Cokey

One Man Went to Mow

Row, Row, Row Your Boat

Skip to My Lou

The More We Get Together

Lavender Blue

Hot Cross Buns

London Bridge Is Falling Down

The Grand Old Duke of York

The I Can't Sing Book

Happy Birthday

In 1893, two kindergarten teachers, sisters Patty and Mildred Hill, wrote a song called "Good Morning to All". The song was published the same year in a collection, *Song Stories for Children*, issued in Chicago by Clayton F. Summy. No one knows who made the slight change in the lyrics to make it a birthday greeting song, but since 1910 not a day has passed that someone, somewhere, hasn't sung "Happy Birthday to You".

Most people think "Happy Birthday" is in the public domain—not so! Clayton F. Summy owns the original copyright, and his company was not above suing the likes of Western Union and Irving Berlin for copyright infringement. Of course, singing the song is not a violation of copyright laws. In fact, "Happy Birthday" is the most frequently sung song in the English language, followed by "Auld Lang Syne". Ironically, the authors not only earned practically nothing from the unprecedented and unequalled success of the song, their names are not even remembered!

Yankee Doodle

Widely regarded as the first American popular song, "Yankee Doodle" was long thought to be of British or German origin. However, research has traced both the words and the music back to the mid-1700's in the American colonies. Whatever its true origin, the song first became popular with the British troops who sang it to poke fun at the colonists. But the Americans liked it and adopted it as their "battle cry".

Music Is...Singing

The words themselves have interesting origins. "Yankee" is thought to be an Indian mispronunciation of the word "English". "Doodle" refers to a foolish fellow or simpleton. A "macaroni" was an 18th century word for a vain person. "Yankee Doodle" was published in London in 1777, the first American song released in Europe. The sheet music instructed the performer that the words were to be "sung through the nose and in the west-country drawl and dialect". No author was credited.

With its snappy beat, this song is great for using rhythm instruments and movement. You can hum the tune through a kazoo or play a drum in time to the music. Sing and march around the room with red, white and blue streamers shaking in the wind.

> Father and I went down to camp
> Along with Captain Gooding,
> And there we saw the men and boys
> As thick as hasty puddin'.
>
> Chorus:
> Yankee Doodle keep it up,
> Yankee Doodle dandy.
> Mind the music and the step
> And with the girls be handy.
>
> And there was Captain Washington,
> Upon a strappin' stallion,
> And all the men and boys around,
> I guess there were a million.
>
> Chorus
>
> Yankee Doodle went to town
> Ridin' on a pony.
> He stuck a feather in his cap,
> And called it macaroni.
>
> Chorus

The I Can't Sing Book

Yankee Doodle Game   2+

TEACHES ABOUT LOUD AND SOFT

Sit on the floor and pretend that you are riding a horse.

Sing the first part of the song in a soft voice.

Sing the chorus in a big voice.

Switch and sing the first part loudly and the second part softly.

The Robin Hood Game   4+

TEACHES CREATIVE DRAMATICS

Talk about Robin Hood and how his outlaws travelled through the woods. When night-time came, they would sing songs around a campfire.

Act out a story where the children go for a walk and stop to build a campfire. Sit in a circle and sing folk songs such as "Robin Hood", "Campfire's Burning" and others.

Activities and Games to Play With Well-Known Songs

Michael, Row the Boat Ashore   2+

TEACHES LANGUAGE DEVELOPMENT

Michael, row the boat ashore, Hallelujah.
Michael, row the boat ashore, Hallelujah.

Change the words of the song to fit the names of the children.

Sing something nice about each one.

Ruthie built a great big tower, Hallelujah.
Victor has a very nice smile, Hallelujah.

● Sing the song about anything!

It is fun to pick up toys, Hallelujah.
Oh, I love my dog so much, Hallelujah.

● This game is a great language booster.

This Old Man 3+

TEACHES COUNTING AND FUN

This old man
He played one.
He played knick, knack on my thumb.
With a knick, knack, paddy whack
Give your dog a bone.
This old man came rolling home.

...two...shoe...
...three...knee...
...four...door...
...five...hive...
...six...sticks...
...seven...heaven...
...eight...gate...
...nine...spine...
...ten...once again...

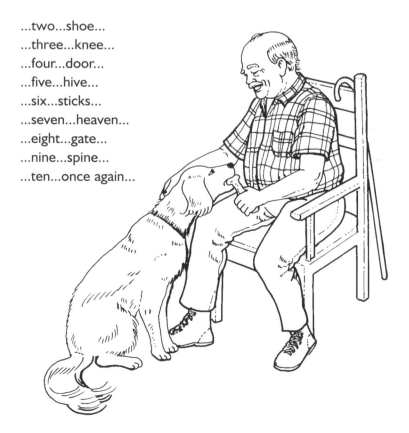

The I Can't Sing Book

● Try this new version of this traditional song. Do all of the movements while standing in place.

This old man, he can shake
Shake, shake, shake while baking a cake. (shake body all over)
With a knick, knack, paddy whack....

This old man, he can kick
Kick, kick, kick just for a trick. (kick each foot one at a time)

This old man, he can twist
Twist, twist, twist and shake your fist. (twist body and shake fist)

This old man, he can run
Run, run, run just for fun. (run in place)

This old man, he can jump
Jump, jump, jump over a bump. (jump in place)

Try making up your own verses.

ABC (Soup) Song   3+

TEACHES ABOUT THE LETTERS OF THE ALPHABET

A B C D E F G
H I J K L M N O P
Q R S T U V
W X Y Z
I've eaten all my A B C's.
May I have some more soup, please?

● Sing the above words to the tune of "Twinkle, Twinkle, Little Star".
Make alphabet cards by writing the letters of the alphabet on index cards with markers. Put the cards in a large soup can. The child takes a card out of the can and names the letter.
Serve alphabet soup or cereal. Put a letter in a spoon and name the letter.

Music Is...Singing

Picture Songs

3

TEACHES SEQUENCING SKILLS

The incy wincy spider (picture of a spider)
   went up the water spout. (picture of a water spout)
Down came the rain and (picture of rain)
   washed the spider out. (picture of spider falling down the spout)
Out came the sun (picture of sun)
   and dried up all the rain. (picture of rainless ground)
And the incy wincy spider went up the spout again. (picture of
   spider going up again)

- Teach "The Incy Wincy Spider" (or any other song) by drawing pictures.
- The words of the song will have more meaning to children, and the visual clues make learning the song easier.
- Other examples of "picture songs" are:

The Wheels on the Bus
The Old Lady Who Swallowed a Fly
Old MacDonald Had a Farm
The Farmer's in his Den
BINGO
If You're Happy and You Know It

Pop Goes the Weasel

3+

DEVELOPS COORDINATION AND THE CONCEPT

OF LOUD AND SOFT

All around the cobbler's bench
The monkey chased the weasel.
The cobbler laughed to see such fun
POP goes the weasel.

- Stoop down low to the ground. Sing the song and on the word "pop" jump up into the air.

The I Can't Sing Book

- Walk around in a circle while singing the song. On the word "pop" fall to the ground.
- One person is the monkey and one person is the weasel. Sing the song as the monkey chases the weasel around the room. On the word "pop" both of you try to get into the same chair.
- Sing all of the words in a very soft voice and sing "pop goes the weasel" in a loud voice.
- Sing the song and clap your hands at the same time. When you come to the last line starting with the word "pop", stamp your feet and clap your hands. You can play this game using many body rhythms—snapping fingers, patting thighs, jumping, hopping, skipping and galloping.
- Use rhythm instruments on the word "pop". This creates great excitement as your child anticipates the word "pop".

The Farmer's in his Den   3+

TEACHES CREATIVITY AND RHYTHMIC MOVEMENT

The farmer's in his den.
The farmer's in his den.
Hi, ho, the derry-o
The farmer's in his den.

- This game is best played with a group of children. Everyone forms a circle. The child chosen to be the farmer stands in the middle of the circle.

- As the song is sung, the other children walk around the circle.
- The farmer chooses someone to be the wife. The two children walk on the inside of the circle and choose another child who could be the cow, the horse, whatever. When everyone has been chosen (make up verses if necessary), the game is over.
- You can change the subject of this song. For example, if you recently went to the zoo, you could sing "The Monkey at the Zoo" and sing about the different animals that you saw at the zoo. To make the game even more fun, sing the song in animal voices and move like the animals.
- Or how about:

> The driver on the bus.
> The driver on the bus.
> Hi, ho, the derry-o
> The driver on the bus.

Here We Go 'Round the Mulberry Bush

3+

TEACHES HOW TO WALK IN A CIRCLE

> Here we go 'round the mulberry bush
> The mulberry bush, the mulberry bush.
> Here we go 'round the mulberry bush,
> So early in the morning.

- Face a child, hold hands and walk in a circle while singing the song. After the first time, reverse the circle and sing the song again.
- If you have several children, choose two of them to be a "bush". Everyone else forms a circle around the "bush" and sings the song.

The I Can't Sing Book

Are You Sleeping?

TEACHES CREATIVITY

Are you sleeping, are you sleeping
Brother John, Brother John?
Morning bells are ringing, morning bells are ringing
Ding ding dong, ding, ding, dong.

- Play this with a group of children.
- Divide the group into two parts. Each group sings and claps the song in a different part of the room.
- Give each group different assignments. One group can sing while the other stamps the song, plays it with rhythm sticks or pats their thighs to the rhythm.
- Sing the song again and give each group a new assignment. Each time you sing the song, move to a different part of the room.

She'll Be Comin' 'Round the Mountain

TEACHES LISTENING SKILLS

She'll be comin' 'round the mountain when she comes.
She'll be comin' 'round the mountain when she comes.
She'll be comin' 'round the mountain, she'll be comin' 'round
   the mountain
She'll be comin' 'round the mountain when she comes.

- This is a great game for a group.
- Sit in a circle either on chairs or on the floor.
- One child is the designated runner.
- As the group sings the song, the runner runs around the outside of the circle.
- On the last word of the song, "comes", the runner stops behind one of the children. This child then becomes the "runner", the first runner sits with the group and the singing begins again.

Singing in pitch is not something you either have or don't have. If you think that you cannot carry a tune it's because someone has told you that and you still believe it. If you practise and try to improve your singing, you can develop your listening skills to a higher level and sing on pitch.

Sing about things you are doing in your house. If you are getting ready to set the table, sing about it as if you are in an opera. "It's time to put the cutlery on the table...here's a bowl, here's a spoon."

chapter 7

Music Is...

Instruments

Have you ever felt the thrill of playing a musical instrument? Did someone ever show you how to play "Chopsticks" on the piano or maybe pluck the strings on a guitar? Imagine how a young child feels when he makes his own instrument and then is able to play it! This is a win-win activity that is as easy as making drums from a coffee can or sewing bells on the fingertips of gloves or on an elastic band to go around the wrist or ankle.

Simple Instruments to Make and Use

Rhythm Sticks

TEACHES EYE-HAND COORDINATION

Materials

Dowels or wooden rulers
Saw

Directions

● Young children will need help. Older children can do most of the work by themselves.
● Cut dowels in 30 cm lengths. You can also use rulers.
● Try cutting notches on the sides of the rulers so when they are rubbed together they make an interesting sound.
● Pencils and sticks also make good rhythm sticks.
● Sing or play music and tap away!

Ribbon Wands
2+

TEACHES MOVING WITH MUSIC

Materials

Paper towel tube
Coloured paper streamers, 18–27 cm long
Stapler

The I Can't Sing Book

Directions

Take a paper towel tube and staple coloured paper streamers to it.

Play music and let your child dance and move the wand in the air.

Things that you can do with the wand:

Make circles in the air over your head and low to the ground

Make different letters and shapes in the air

Move the wand back and forth like a windscreen wiper

Easy Shakers

2+

TEACHES RHYTHM EXPRESSION

Materials

Aluminium pie dish or paper plates

Rocks, dried beans (or any other "shakeable" material)

Stapler

Directions

Shakers can be made from pie dishes or paper plates filled with rocks or dried beans and stapled together.

Sea shells filled with tiny pebbles and taped together or held together by rubber bands also make good shakers.

Dried beans or stones in old medicine bottles make different sounds.

Shake the shaker high in the sky and low to the ground.

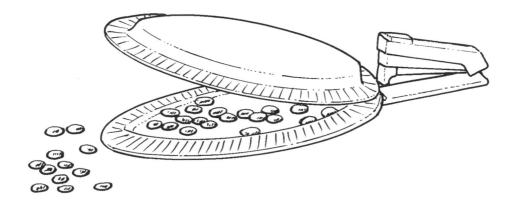

Large Bell Shakers

Materials

Plastic milk bottle with a handle (use different sizes)
Jingle bells
Colourful wooden or plastic beads
Stickers
Glue
Heavy tape

Directions

- Put some bells and beads into the plastic milk bottle. Young children love doing this and it develops their eye-hand coordination.
- Put some glue inside the cap and screw on tightly. Also reinforce the lid with heavy tape for safety.
- Encourage children to put stickers on the plastic milk bottle for decorations.
- Sing and shake to your favourite tune.

Paper Plate Tambourine

Materials

Strong paper plate
3 or 4 jingle bells
String or wool
Markers, crayons,
   stickers, glitter, etc,
   optional

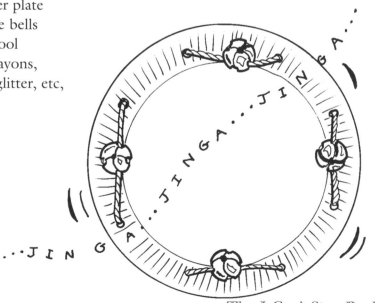

The I Can't Sing Book

Directions

Punch holes around the edge of the paper plate.

Thread the string or wool through the holes to attach the bells around the plate.

Decorate the paper plate with markers, crayons, stickers, glitter, etc.

Show your child how you can shake the tambourine or tap it with your hand.

Play music or sing a song as you play the tambourine.

Snare Drum   3+

TEACHES SOUND DISCRIMINATION

Materials

A metal container, such as a biscuit tin

Several metal paper clips

Cardboard

Scissors

Masking tape

Glitter and glue, stickers or acrylic paint pens, optional

Wooden spoons, chopsticks or pencils

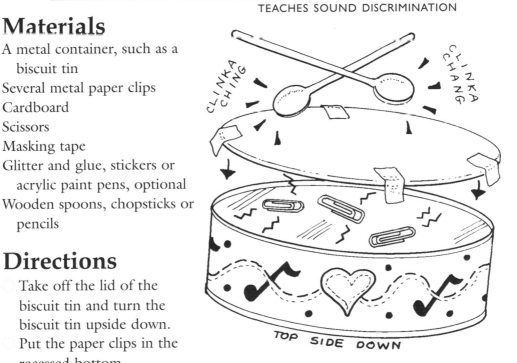

Directions

Take off the lid of the biscuit tin and turn the biscuit tin upside down.

Put the paper clips in the recessed bottom.

Cut a cardboard circle a little larger than the bottom of the biscuit tin and place it over the bottom of the biscuit tin. Secure the cardboard with masking tape.

Decorate the drum with glitter, stickers or acrylic paint pens. If it is a Christmas tin, it probably has nice decorations already.

- Give your child some wooden spoons, chopsticks or pencils to play the drum.
- The paper clips give the drum the metallic sound similar to a snare drum.

Bongos

TEACHES RHYTHM

Materials

2 empty plastic bleach or fabric conditioner bottles, preferably different sizes
Scissors
Heavy tape, such as duct tape
Staples and a stapler
Colourful plastic tape and stickers

Directions

- Cut off the tops of the bleach bottles evenly.
- Cover the cut edge of the bottles with duct tape to protect little fingers.
- Staple the bottles together and cover the staples with heavy tape.
- Decorate the bongos with colourful tape and stickers.
- Sit on the floor with the bongos between your legs.
- Play the bongos along with singing or listening to a recording. If you have two sizes, you will be able to hear a difference in the sound.

BA - DA - BA   BOP BOP BOP

② tape edges

① cut off tops

③ staple and tape

④ decorate and play!

The I Can't Sing Book

Maracas

TEACHES LISTENING SKILLS

Used to make lively music, authentic maracas are made from dried, hard-shelled fruit called gourds, which are filled with seeds or small stones.

Materials

Film containers
Popcorn kernels, rice or beans
Glue
Knife
Lollipop sticks
Spray paint or musical stickers, optional

④ put stick in slit

③ slit lid

① fill ¼ full

② glue + close lid

GLUE

¼

⑤ decorate and ≥ SHAKE ≤

RATTLE

POP

Directions

Fill one-quarter of each container with the popcorn kernels (or rice or beans).
Place a little glue on the inside of the lid and close tightly.
Take a knife and make a small slit in the lid.
Put the lollipop stick inside the slit.
If desired, spray paint these and put stickers on for decorations.
Sing a song and shake these instruments to the rhythm.

Tin Can Bell

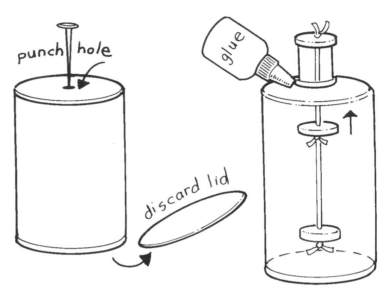

Materials

An aluminium soup can with one end removed (make sure open end
  doesn't have any sharp edges)
Hammer and nail
2 large buttons
Wool or string
An empty cotton reel
Glue

Directions

- Punch a hole in the end of the can using a hammer and a nail.
- Thread one button through the string and tie a knot at one end.
- Thread the second button through the string and tie another knot
  below it, as shown.
- Thread the string through the hole in the can.
- Put glue on the top of the can.
- Thread the string through the cotton reel and tie securely around
  the top so that the cotton reel is pushed tightly against the top of
  the can in the glue. (Allow the glue to dry before using.)

The I Can't Sing Book

Flower Pot Bells   3+

Materials
Different sizes of clay flower pots, three is a good number
Heavy cord cut into pieces long enough to tie to a tree branch
A wooden spoon

Directions

- Make a large knot at one end of each piece of cord.
- Put the cord through the flower pot hole and tie the other end to a heavy tree branch or something to suspend the pot in the air.
- Tap the pots with the wooden spoon and listen to the different sounds that you can produce.
- Point out that the smaller pots make a higher sound and the larger pots make a lower sound.

Cymbals   3+

Cymbals are wonderful instruments for developing fine motor skills and eye-hand coordination. Many years ago, the English called them "clash-pans", which was hitting two pot covers together. Cymbals can be large and small. The small ones are often used in Greek dancing, the large ones in symphony orchestras.

Materials

2 aluminium pie dishes
Hammer and nail
Paper towel tube
Scissors
2 paper fasteners
Stickers or enamel spray
   paint, optional

Directions

- With the hammer and nail, punch a hole in the centre of each pie dish.
- Cut the toilet roll tube in quarters and using the paper fasteners, fasten a quarter to each one of the pie dishes.
- If desired, decorate with stickers or enamel paint.
- Sing a song and at the end of each line, clash the cymbals.
- Finger cymbals can be made by punching two holes in each of two bottle caps. Then thread the caps with a loop of elastic or a rubber band. Slide one cymbal on your thumb and one on your second finger. Clap them together.

The Hotchy Potchy   3+

DEVELOPS IMAGINATION

Materials

Broom stick
Assorted objects such as bells, aluminium pie dishes, rattles, keys,
   spoons, wind chimes, containers filled with stones
Tape, glue, wire, heavy staple, nails to attach objects to the broom stick
Rubber chair cup

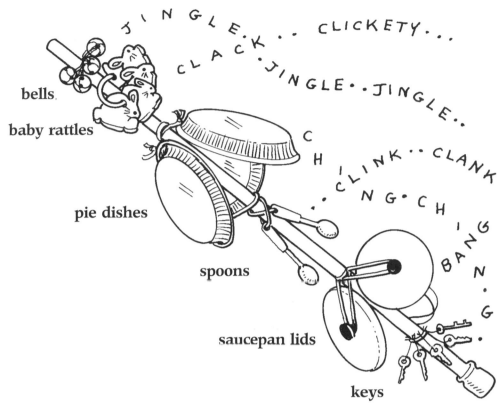

JINGLE...CLICKETY...CLACK..JINGLE..JINGLE..CLINK..CLANK..CHING·CHING·CHBANG·N·G

bells

baby rattles

pie dishes

spoons

saucepan lids

keys

Directions

● This instrument can have any name that you desire. I've seen it called a Boombah, a Jangle Stick and a Rattler.

Use a broom stick or a pogo stick. Some broom sticks have springs on them and this is ideal. You can also use a child's broomstick.

Attach the noisemakers to the stick with heavy staples (with wooden broomsticks), telephone wires, rope or twine, nails or duct tape.

Noisemaker suggestions are bells, aluminium pie dishes, keys, rattles, containers filled with rice or stones, two spoons tied together and wind chimes.

Put a rubber chair cup on the end of the stick.

Take the stick with the attachments and hit it on the floor to the beat of the music. If the Hotchy Potchy does not have a rubber "foot", stomp it in a box or a wooden crate.

The sound is fun. Play it to your favourite song.

This instrument has so many possibilities. It gives children a chance to experiment with many sounds. It's a highly creative activity.

Music Is...Instruments

Water Bells

Materials

5 water glasses all the same size, at least 15 cm tall
Water in a jug
Ruler
A metal spoon

Directions

- Place the glasses in a row.
- Pour the water into each glass as follows: the first glass, 2.5 cm; the second glass, 5 cm; and so on, filling up the fifth glass 12.5 cm.
- Gently tap the glasses with the spoon and you should hear the first five notes of the major scale—doh, ray, me, fah, soh.
- If you play the first three glasses starting with the third glass you will play the beginning of the song "Mary Had a Little Lamb". Here is the order of the glasses you will play:

3	2	1	2	3	3	3
Ma	ry	had	a	lit	tle	lamb

- Experiment with the sounds by adding water and decreasing the water. When you add more water, the sound will be higher and when you decrease the water, the sound will be lower.
- If you use coloured water, you will have rainbow music.

Bottle-Top Castanets

Materials

2 bottle tops
Nail
Hammer
A strip of cardboard 15 cm long, folded in half
String or wool

The I Can't Sing Book

Directions

- Punch a hole into the centre of each bottle top with a hammer and nail.
- Make similar holes in the cardboard strip 2.5 cm from each end.
- Place each bottle top as shown over a cardboard hole and push the string through both holes and knot the ends tightly.
- Let your child have one or two castanets. Show her how to hold a castanet in her hand and click the two parts together.
- Play some music with a Spanish flavour and dance and click the castanets. Say, "Olé!"

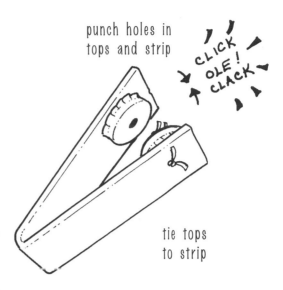

punch holes in tops and strip

CLICK OLÉ! CLACK

tie tops to strip

Box Banjo

4+

TEACHES RHYTHM

Materials

2 Styrofoam produce or meat trays
Scissors
Glue
Rubber bands of different widths
Stickers, tempera paint and brushes (optional)

Directions

- Cut a 5 cm x 10 cm rectangular piece from the middle of one tray.
- Glue the two trays together as shown in the illustration.
- Stretch the rubber bands across the opening. Use different size rubber bands to achieve different sounds: the thinner the band, the higher the sound.
- Decorate the boxes.
- Strum the banjos as you sing your favourite song.

Easy Kazoos   4+

The kazoo is one of the simplest instruments that plays a melody. The music is produced by humming a melody into the kazoo, which causes the vibrating membrane to produce a musical sound. It is a perfect instrument for a young child.

Materials

Toilet roll tubes
Markers
Coloured
    cellophane or grease
    proof paper cut into
    10 cm squares
Rubber bands

Directions

- Decorate the tubes.
- Attach a cellophane square to one end of the tube with a rubber band.
- Hum your favourite tune into the other end of the tube.
- Beware! This will tickle your upper lip.

A comb kazoo —Wrap a piece of grease proof paper around a comb and secure it with two-sided tape. Put your kazoo next to your lips and hum your favourite song. Be prepared! It, too, will tickle your mouth.

The I Can't Sing Book

Recorder

4+

TEACHES IMAGINATION

This instrument will look like a recorder but you play it like a kazoo.

Materials

Paper towel roll
Aluminium foil
Cone-shaped paper
   drinking cup
Tape
Small dot stickers

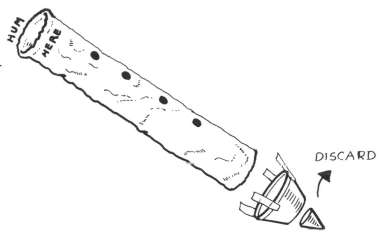

Directions

● Cover the paper
   towel roll with
   aluminium foil.
   Bring all the
   excess up at one end to form a mouthpiece. Make sure that the
   mouthpiece has an opening for the child to hum into.
● Cut off the triangle end of the paper cup and attach it to the bottom
   end of the tube with tape.
● Place the stickers on the instrument to represent the keys.
● Pretend to play the recorder while humming your favourite tune.

Waffle Harps or Kazoos   **4+**

TEACHES ABOUT VIBRATION

Materials

2 tongue depressors
3 wide, large rubber bands

Directions

- Wrap one rubber band around a tongue depressor the long way.
- Put second tongue depressor on top of the first one.
- Take the second rubber band and twist it once around one depressor. Continue twisting the second rubber band around both depressors.
- Take the third rubber band and repeat the above step, remembering to twist around one depressor one time and then around both.
- There will be a small opening at each end of the depressors. Blow or hum gently into the middle of the depressors.
- Make up your own tune or play along to a familiar tune.

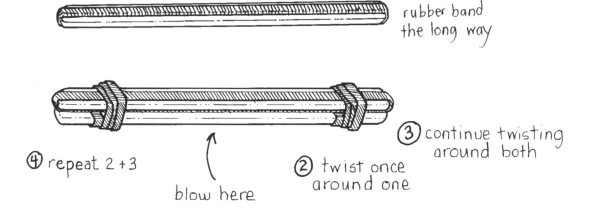

① wrap a rubber band the long way

③ continue twisting around both

④ repeat 2 + 3

blow here

② twist once around one

Drum Necklace

TEACHES MOVING TO A BEAT

Materials

- One coffee can with both ends removed
- Duct tape
- Hammer and nail
- 2 coffee can plastic lids
- Ribbon
- Enamel spray paint or stickers, optional

The I Can't Sing Book

Directions

- Cover any sharp can edges with duct tape.
- Punch a hole into the centre of each plastic lid.
- Pass the ribbon through the hole and knot on the inside of the lid. Repeat with the other lid.
- Place the lids on the coffee can drum. The ribbon is the necklace.
- You can decorate the coffee cans in advance or spray with enamel paint. You can also decorate with stickers.
- Put the drum over your head and hit the ends of the drum with your hands or a rhythm stick.
- Little children love having their own drum to march and dance with.

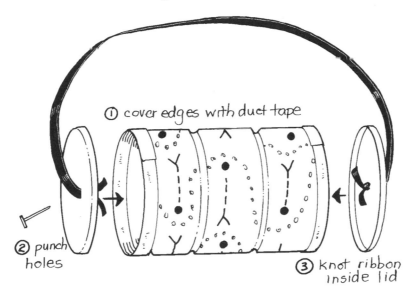

Rhythm Instrument Games

Playing an instrument is like making a machine work. You are attached to your body, so when you clap your hands or tap your feet, you are making rhythm with your body. When you play an instrument, you are making something else work that is not attached to your body. This takes another level of cognitive thinking and coordination. Playing an instrument also develops fine motor and listening skills and instils a sense of pride in a young child.

Traditional rhythm instruments for children

Sand blocks
Cymbals
Castanets
Rhythm sticks
Maracas
Tone blocks (also known
as "tick tocks")

Tambourine
Triangle
Bells
Drums
Xylophone

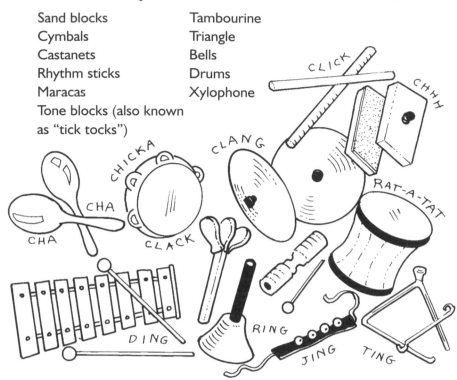

Rhythm Stick Ideas   1+

INTRODUCES YOUNG CHILDREN TO A

SIMPLE MUSICAL INSTRUMENT

- Rhythm sticks are an excellent instrument for young children because they are easy to play.
- Rhythm sticks develop fine motor skills, eye-hand coordination and listening skills.
- There are three kinds of rhythm sticks.

> A stick with a smooth surface, about 15 cm in length. When you hit two together you will hear a smooth sound.
>
> A stick that has a grooved (fluted) surface. When played with another stick and rubbed against another stick, you will hear a scratching sound.
>
> A shorter and fatter stick. Excellent for small hands. This stick is called a "lummi stick".

● Use rhythm sticks for specific reasons, not only to "hit your sticks to the music". Rhythm sticks can be used to highlight certain rhythm parts of a song, as a substitution for the words and as an accompaniment to a familiar song.

Rhythm Stick Games 2+

1. Pop Goes the Weasel

Sing the song and hit your sticks on "pop". Hide the sticks behind your back until it's time to "pop!"

2. One, Two, Three, Four

Hit the sticks in rhythm to the following poem:

> One, two, three, four
> Who's that knocking on my door?
> Five, six, seven, eight
> Hurry up, I just can't wait.

You can hit the sticks on every word, at the end of each line, etc. Make up different ways to hit the sticks to the poem.

3. Follow the Beat

Use a metronome or a timer with this game. Sit on the floor and hit your sticks in time with the beat. Vary the speed of the timer. Make up stories to go with the various speeds. Fast speeds can be animals scampering through the woods. Slow speeds can be bears and elephants lumbering through the woods.

4. B-I-N-G-O

Try tapping a rhythm stick to the song "BINGO". Tap the stick on the floor to the letters B-I-N-G-O. Instead of singing the letters, hit your sticks. This is fun and takes a lot of eye-hand coordination.

5. Tap or Wait

Tap the sticks on the floor and say the word "tap" each time you hit the stick on the floor or table. When you say the word "wait" do not hit the stick. Try "tap, tap, tap, wait". This means you will hit the sticks three times and wait on the last time. Try "tap-wait, tap-wait". After your child can do these patterns easily, try saying the words to yourself so that all you can hear is the tapping.

Oh, When the Band Comes Marching In

2+

● Sing the following words to the tune of "When the Saints Go Marching In".

> Oh, when the band comes marching in.
> Oh, when the band comes marching in.
> I want to sing and play to the music,
> When the band comes marching in.

● Let your child pick a rhythm instrument to play as she marches around the room to the music.
● Play some other march music and let your child march to the music. Anything by John Philip Sousa works wonderfully.

Colours and Instruments

2+

TEACHES ABOUT STOP AND GO

● Give your child his favourite rhythm instrument.
● If he chooses bells, show him how to stop the sound of bells by putting one palm over the other palm holding the bells, like putting a blanket over the bells.
● You will need two pieces of paper—one red and one green.

The I Can't Sing Book

When you hold up the green paper, it's time to play the instrument.
When you hold up the red paper, it's time to stop playing the
instrument.

Sing the following to the tune of "London Bridge".

> Now it's time to hold up green, hold up green, hold up green.
> Now it's time to hold up green.
> Play, play the music.
>
> Now it's time to hold up red, hold up red, hold up red.
> Now it's time to hold up red.
> No more music.

After playing this game a few times, relate it to red and green lights
you see when you are driving in the car.

Rhythm Stick Sounds   3+

TEACHES ABOUT LOUD AND SOFT SOUNDS

This game teaches the concept of loud and soft. We all make loud
and soft noises all of the time but might not be aware of it.

Take a rhythm stick and demonstrate the game. Hit the stick loudly
on the floor three times. Each time you hit the stick say, "Loud,
loud, loud".

● Hit the stick softly on the floor three times. Each time you hit the
stick softly, say, "Soft, soft, soft".

Hit the stick and say the words with your child several times.

Try saying the word "loud" in a loud voice and the word "soft" in a
soft voice.

Ask your child to guess if you are hitting the stick loudly or softly.

Use other instruments to make the loud and soft sounds. Drums,
tone block and tambourines work well.

Playing With Rhythm Sticks   3+

TEACHES COUNTING SKILLS AND COORDINATION

● The song "This Old Man" is excellent for rhythm experiences. Sit on the floor with your child and give him a rhythm stick.

● Sing the first verse of "This Old Man".

> This old man, he played one. (hit the stick on the floor one time)
> He played knick knack on my thumb.
> With a knick knack paddy whack
> Give your dog a bone.
> This old man came rolling home.

● Continue singing the song and after each number, hit the stick on the floor and count out the number.

> ...one...thumb...
> ...two...shoe...
> ...three...knee...
> ...four...door...
> ...five...hive...

Twinkle, Twinkle, Little Stick   3+

TEACHES LISTENING SKILLS

● Sing the following to the tune of "Twinkle, Twinkle, Little Star".

> Twinkle, twinkle, little stick
> Some are thin and some are thick.
> When I hold you in my hand
> I pretend I lead the band.
> Twinkle, twinkle, little stick
> I'm so glad I know this trick.
>
> Jackie Silberg

● The child taps the stick as you sing the song together.
● Try tapping the stick on different surfaces as you sing the song.
● Let your child pretend to be a conductor as you sing.

       The I Can't Sing Book

Percussion Games 3+

Drums

Play a drum loud, soft, fast and slow. Let your child dance to the loud music, soft music, then fast and slow. If you strike the drum around the edges, it will have a higher sound than if you strike it in the middle. This is because the skin of the drum is looser in the middle and therefore the vibration is slower.

Tone Blocks

Tone blocks are very subtle instruments. A tone block is made up of two parts. When you strike it, you will get a different tone on each side of the block. This is because one side is thicker than the other. Tone blocks are perfect for teaching your child tone discrimination. They are often called "tick tocks" because they sound like a clock ticking.

Bells, Maracas and Tambourines

These are similar instruments. With each one you can vary the speed, intensity and rhythm to play games in which your child listens for high and low sounds, fast and slow sounds, and loud and soft sounds. You can also play counting games, for example, asking your child to shake the maraca four times.

Drum Beats 3+

DEVELOPS LISTENING SKILLS

Play different rhythms on a hand drum. You can also use a wooden spoon on a metal pot.

Start with a steady beat and ask your child to walk to the drum beat. Tell her that when the drum stops, she should stop walking.

Add a new rhythm; play faster, telling your child to run to the rhythm. When the drum stops, she can stop.

Now alternate the two rhythms and help your child listen and decide if she should walk or run.

- Play other rhythms and attach them to a movement. For example, a loud and soft beat could be for hopping. A swishing sound could be for sliding. A very soft beat could be for tiptoeing.
- This is an excellent game to develop auditory awareness.

Can You Cuckoo With Your Kazoo?   3+

TEACHES COUNTING SKILLS

- Say the following poem, "The Cuckoo Bird", and tap your sticks on the words "tick-tock".

> Tick-tock, tick-tock, where's the cuckoo bird?
> Tick-tock, tick-tock, when will he be heard?
> Tick-tock, tick-tock, the minutes tick away.
> Tick-tock, tick-tock, listen and he'll say,
> Cuckoo, cuckoo, cuckoo.
>> Jackie Silberg

- When you say the word "cuckoo" try saying it with a kazoo.
- Tell your child that it is a certain time and let her "cuckoo" that number. If it is three o'clock, she will "cuckoo" three times.

Musical Mobile   3+

TEACHES THE NAMES OF MUSICAL INSTRUMENTS

- You can find packages of miniature musical instruments in a school supply store or toy shop.
- Tie the individual instruments to a coat hanger for a mobile.
- Play the following game with your child. Sing to the tune of "Twinkle, Twinkle, Little Star".

The I Can't Sing Book

Music Everywhere

I hear music everywhere,
Lovely sounds that fill the air.
Where's the music coming from,
Instruments that sing and hum?
Find an instrument today
That you can pretend to play.
Jackie Silberg

● Ask your child to touch one of the instruments on the mobile.
● Pretend to play that instrument or make the sound of the chosen instrument.

Imagination with Instruments 3+

DEVELOPS CREATIVITY

● Use instruments to produce sound effects for stories and poems, and make up stories to go with the sounds of the instruments.

Sand block—trains
Triangle—tinkly sounds like fairies and elves
Tone block—clock ticking

● If you don't have access to instruments, try using simple kitchen utensils—spoons (metal and wood), egg beaters and brushes on pots.
● Try this:

The incy wincy spider went up the waterspout. (go up the scale on a xylophone or hit two sticks together)
Down came the rain and washed the spider out. (go down the scale on the xylophone or hit two cymbals together)
Out came the sun and dried up all the rain. (use the triangle or clink two metal spoons together lightly)
And the incy wincy spider went up the spout again. (go up the scale on a xylophone or hit two sticks together)

Bye, Bye Earth   3+

● Say the following rhyme and then take rhythm instruments and make space music. Start with a loud sound as the spaceship blasts off into space. The further away from earth the spaceship travels, the softer it will sound on earth. Pretend to be floating in space and play "tinkly" music.

> One is one and two is two,
> I'm an astronaut, who are you?
>
> Three is three and four is four,
> Listen to my capsule roar.
>
> Five is five, and six is six,
> Into space, it's very quick.
>
> Seven is seven and eight is eight,
> Very soon we'll have no weight.
>
> Nine is nine and ten is ten,
> Let's go back to earth again.
>   Jackie Silberg

● Play the instruments again as you fly back to earth.

Hey Mr Monday   3+

TEACHES THE DAYS OF THE WEEK AND

ENCOURAGES CREATIVITY

● Sit on the floor with your child. Each child is assigned a day of the week. If there are more than seven children, more than one child can be assigned each day. If there are fewer than seven children, one child can take more than one day.

● Each of you holds a rhythm instrument in your hands.

● Say, "Hey Mr Monday, play a tune for me".

● Encourage him to play his instrument in any way that he desires.

● Now say, "Hey Mr Tuesday, play a tune for me".

● You play on your instrument.

- Continue taking turns and naming the days of the week.
- If you are playing different instruments, switch.
- Add other directions. "Play a soft song for me", etc.

Tell a Tale of Rhythm   4+

DEVELOPS IMAGINATION AND LISTENING SKILLS

- Tapping rhythm sticks (or wooden spoons) on different surfaces will produce many different sounds. Ask your child to identify what he thinks the noise sounds like. For example:

  > Table top—sounds like raindrops
  > Floor—sounds like a hammer
  > Window (very gently!)—sounds like a woodpecker
  > Metal—sounds like echoes in a tunnel
  > Shoe—sounds like a tap dripping

- Pick three different sounds and make up a story using the names of the sounds. For example: One day the sky grew dark and it started to rain. (Make the sound of raindrops with your sticks.) Andrew (or other child's name) went outside to put his toys away and he heard a rat-a-tat-tat on the tree in his yard. He looked closely and saw a woodpecker (tap the sticks on the window), etc.
- Tell a familiar fairy tale to your child and choose different places to use the sticks. The story of the "The Three Bears" is a good one to use; tap the sticks on different surfaces to represent each bear.

A recent study done by neurologist Frank Wilson showed that when a musician plays music, he uses approximately 90 percent of the brain. Wilson could find no other activity that uses the brain to this extent. Therefore, he concluded that a child who is playing a musical instrument or singing on a regular basis is exercising the entire brain.

Research on the arts shows us that children with poorly developed academic skills succeed with school-related skills through experiences with art and dance.

chapter 8

• Music Is...

Fun-filled Activities

Musical activities can include listening to the rhythm of a dripping tap, marching to a metronome, identifying sounds on a tape recorder, imitating environmental sounds, making up silly words to a song and more. Through music we can express thoughts, feelings, moods, emotions and creativity. Especially in early childhood, children feel free to interpret music in their own ways. This includes composing new verses, melodies or creative movements to songs. When children sing, dance, move and have rhythm experiences or use a combination of these activities, they learn maths and language skills, creativity, coordination and other important skills and concepts. Because they are learning by doing, they internalize the concepts and their learning skills are enhanced.

Fun-filled Activities and Games That Teach Skills and Concepts

Change the Words   2+

DEVELOPS LANGUAGE AND CREATIVITY

- Remember in *Alice in Wonderland* by Lewis Carroll how the words of "Twinkle, Twinkle, Little Star" were changed to "Twinkle, Twinkle, Little Bat?" Changing the words to familiar songs is a wonderful way to develop creativity.
- Choose a song that your child knows well. Familiar songs like "Old MacDonald", "The Wheels on the Bus" and "Skip to My Lou" are good to use.
- Try singing "Old MacDonald Had a Supermarket" and sing about all the items in the supermarket. Make up a sound to go with the food.

      orange juice—slurp, slurp
      celery—crunch, crunch
      raisins—yum, yum

- For "The Wheels on the Bus" name animals that are on the bus.

      sheep on the bus go "baa, baa, baa"
      cows on the bus go "moo, moo, moo"
      dinosaurs on the bus go "grrr, grrr, grrr"

- "Skip to My Lou" is fun to sing. Instead of "flies in the buttermilk" change the insect and the liquid.

      bees in the milkshake
      grasshoppers in the apple juice

- This is a lot of fun. Be prepared for laughs and giggles.

The I Can't Sing Book

Oh, John the Rabbit

2+

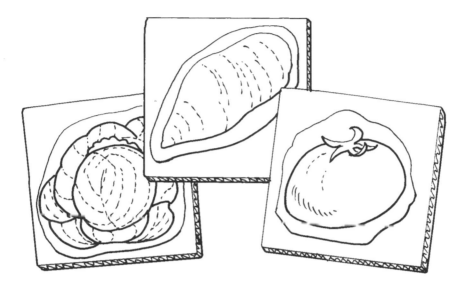

- Make vegetable cards by cutting out pictures and pasting them on sturdy cardboard.
- Ask the children to sit in a circle and give each child a card.
- Teach the following rhythmic poem. The teacher says the words and the children say "yes, ma'am".

> Oh, John the rabbit—yes ma'am
> Got a funny habit—yes ma'am
> Jumping in my garden—yes ma'am
> Cutting down my cabbage—yes ma'am
> My juicy carrots—yes ma'am
> My fresh tomatoes—yes ma'am
> And if I live—yes ma'am
> To see next spring—yes ma'am
> I'm not going to have—yes ma'am
> Any veggies to bring—yes ma'am

- Discuss the vegetables in the poem and how they grow in a garden.
- Choose one child to be "John, the rabbit". Give this child a basket and let him hop around the circle collecting all of the vegetables while you say the poem again.

Music Is...Fun-filled Activities

Guess the Word

3+

- Whistle, hum or play a favourite song.
- Ask your child to guess the song.
- Whistle, hum or play the song again but this time stop on a certain word and ask your child to identify the word.
- A good way to start this game is to stop on the last word of each line. For example, "Twinkle, twinkle, little _____". Let your child fill in the word "star".

Mr Billy Goat

3+

- The story of "The Three Billy Goats Gruff" is a favourite with little children. The following listening game is very popular.
- Sing the following words to the tune of "Ring a Ring o' Rosies".

> Oh, Mr Billy Goat
> May I cross your bridge?

- Mr Billy Goat answers, "You may cross my bridge, if you ask in a soft voice."
- This time ask, "Oh, Mr Billy Goat, may I cross your bridge?" in a soft voice.
- Mr Billy Goat answers, "You may cross my bridge, if you ask in a high voice."
- Continue playing the game. Whatever kind of voice Mr Billy Goat requests, reply with that voice.
- Mr Billy Goat can ask you to say the words in a low voice, fast voice, slow voice, soft voice, sad voice, silly voice, squeaky voice, cackling voice, etc.
- At any time, Mr Billy Goat can say, "Yes, now you may cross the bridge." When Mr Billy Goat is speaking, he uses the voice that he wants the children to use.

The I Can't Sing Book

Bell Horses

DEVELOPS COUNTING SKILLS

Bell horses, bell horses, what's the time of day?
1 o'clock, 2 o'clock, time to go away.
Good horses, bad horses, what's the time of day?
3 o'clock, 4 o'clock, time to go away.

● Sing the above song while holding your child's hand. Gently hold up one of the child's fingers on "1 o'clock", then hold up a second finger on "2 o'clock", and so on.
● This activity can reinforce counting skills and begins to teach children how to tell time if you show your child a clock with hands. Move the little hand to 1 on "1 o'clock", to 2 on "2 o'clock", etc, while you sing the song.
● Move to the beat with any part of the body—clap, sway, nod your head, etc.
● Make a "clip-clop" sound with your tongue; encourage your child to make the same sound.

Up and Down Beauty

3+

TEACHES LISTENING SKILLS

● Play instrumental music that goes up and down a lot. Any Mozart or Haydn symphony would be perfect.
● As you listen to the music with your child, move your hand up when the music goes up and move your hand down when the music goes down.
● Give your child some paper and crayons and let her draw up and down lines as she listens to the music.
● Remember that listening time should be about three or four minutes.
● Hang that beautiful picture for all the world to see!

We Are Fine Musicians 3+

TEACHES THE CONCEPT OF "NEAR" AND "FAR"

- This is a traditional song. If you don't know the melody, either make up your own tune or say the words.
- Talk about "far" and "near". Do objects change in size when they are far away? Why do things look larger when they are near? Talk about how sounds are softer when they are far away.
- Divide the group of children into two parts.
- Line up half of the musicians at one side of the room and let them march towards the other half of the group on the other side of the room while singing the following song.

> Oh, we are fine musicians, we come from far away.
> Oh, we are fine musicians, we come from far away.
> We sing and play and sing and play.
> We clap and tap and clap and tap.
> Oh, we are fine musicians, we come from far away.

- Ask them to start singing softly and gradually get louder as they get closer to the other half of the class. You may need to direct the loud and soft singing.
- After each group has had a turn singing, pass out rhythm instruments and play the game again, this time adding rhythm instrument playing to the singing.

136   The I Can't Sing Book

The Conductor Game 3+

The conductor of an orchestra is the leader, the person in charge, the boss. The conductor controls how fast or slow the music is played, how loud or soft the music is played, and the beat (the steady rhythm).

The players in the orchestra must watch the conductor so that everyone can play the music the same way and all together.

Some conductors use a baton to conduct. The baton is a short, thin stick. Other conductors use their hands to conduct the music.

Children love to play conductor because it lets them feel powerful.

The conductor says:

> I am the conductor
> Of this great big band.
> You can play the music
> If you watch my hand.

Play some music and let your child conduct the music.

After you have done this a few times, show your little maestro some things she can do with her hands to tell the members of the band how to play the music.

> Loudly—put both hands in front of your face with your palms facing your mouth. Shake your hands in front of your face.
> Softly—put your fingers to your mouth in a "shhh" motion.
> Fast and slow—move your baton or hands fast or slowly.

If you have a group of children, pass out rhythm instruments and let the children take turns being the conductor.

Learning should be fun. I've found that the more fun involved in the learning process, the more the children will learn.

Tape Recorder Games   3+

Here are sound games that you can play using a tape recorder.

Mystery Sound

● Pick three sounds and put them on tape, for example, door slamming, water running and radio playing. Say to your child, "I'm thinking of something that _____." Describe one of the sounds. Play the tape and ask your child to tell you when she hears the sound that you described.

Identifying Sounds

● Record five sounds on a tape recorder, for example, doorbell ringing, typing on a keyboard, playing a drum, laughing and whispering.
● Play all of the sounds and let the children listen to them.
● Now, play the first sound and ask, "Where would you hear this sound?" and "Who (or what) makes this sound?"

A Sequence Game

● Record three sounds on a tape recorder.
● Play the sounds for your child and talk about each one as you listen to the sound.
● Ask your child which sound was first, second and third.
● Listen to the sounds again and instead of naming the sounds, act them out as you hear them.
● Ask your child again to tell you which sound was first, second and third. (With older children you can add three new sounds to act out.) This game is great for teaching sequencing skills.

Story Sounds

● Tape a group of sounds that pertain to the same subject. Sounds from school, home and outside are good ones to start with.
● Play the sounds for your child and be sure that he can identify them.
● Make up a story to go with the sounds. This is a very creative game. For an extra challenge, each time you play the sounds, make up a new story.

A Singing Game

The next time that you are going to teach a song to your child, record yourself singing the song.

Play the recording and clap your hands to the music as you listen to your own voice.

Try playing a drum as you listen to your recording.

Now suggest that your child make a recording.

Tape Talk

This is a game that you can play with your child or that your child can play by herself.

Make a tape that gives instructions for moving different parts of her body. Here are some ideas.

Sing the instructions to the tune of "Mary Had a Little Lamb".

> Now it's time to raise one hand, raise one hand, raise one hand.
> Now it's time to raise one hand
> One, two, stop.

Continue with different directions, always ending with "one, two, stop".

Other ideas are: now it's time to wiggle your toes, now it's time to make a fist, now it's time to shake your thumb, now it's time to bend your elbows.

Make up your own ideas too.

This game develops coordination and listening skills.

Metronome Games 3+

● What is a metronome? It is a rhythm counter. It comes in all shapes and sizes and can be electric, battery operated or wind up. When you turn it on, you will hear a steady beat. You can change the beat to very fast or very slow. Musicians use metronomes for practising so that they can keep an even tempo. These are wonderful games to play with a metronome.

The Metronome March

● Turn on the metronome and walk or march to the beat. This takes a lot of listening skills and children really enjoy doing this. Make the beat go faster and when you do, you can change the movement. Hopping, skipping, jumping and tiptoeing are good ideas.

A Counting Game

● Set the beat at a slow pace and tell your child that you are going to count to four. Count on each beat and turn off the metronome after you have said "four". Keep counting higher depending on the age of your child.

● Remember, this game is to help a child develop a sense of rhythm, not learn how to count.

● Try this game naming colours or animals on the beat.

The I Can't Sing Book

Count the Word

DEVELOPS LISTENING AND COUNTING SKILLS

Pick a song that repeats the same word several times, for example, "Mary Had a Little Lamb".

Ask your child to count the number of times the word "lamb" is sung.

Sing the song again (one person sings, the other counts).

How many times was the word sung?

Change the Singer

DEVELOPS LISTENING AND THINKING SKILLS

This game takes a lot of concentration and careful listening.

Start by alternating lines of a song with your child.

> You sing: The wheels on the bus go round and round, round and round, round and round.
> Child sings: The wheels on the bus go round and round, all through the town.

Make it a little harder.

> You sing: The wheels on the bus go
> Child sings: Round and round, round and round, round and round
> You sing: The wheels on the bus go
> Child sings: Round and round
> You sing: All through the
> Child sings: town

Each song that you choose can be manipulated in various ways. You can decide, based on the age of your child.

The hardest thing to do is to alternate words. You might even try it with another adult to discover how very difficult it can be.

In 1993 a pilot study was conducted at the University of California, Irvine, by Frances Rauscher, Ph.D and assistant Gordon Shaw, Ph.D, also of the University of California. Ten three year olds were given music training, either singing or keyboard lessons. The scores of every child improved significantly (46%) on the Object Assembly Task, a section of the Wechsler Preschool and Primary Scale of Intelligence that measures spatial reasoning. In a second experiment, it was found that the spatial reasoning performance of preschool children who received eight months of music lessons far exceeded that of a comparable group who did not receive the music lessons.

chapter 9

Music Is...

a Great Way to Teach

Music makes children happy. Here are 20 musical ideas to use throughout the year. (No prior training necessary.) Promise to try at least three!

20 Musical Ideas

1. Let each child bring in a favourite cassette (or CD). This gives the child a feeling of worth and the adult an insight into what the child likes.

2. Tape familiar sounds. The playground, children talking, traffic outside, teachers' voices. Play "Name the Sound". Ask the children to identify the sounds on the tape. This is a great game for developing listening skills.

3. Sing sequential songs to develop reading skills. "The Old Lady Who Swallowed a Fly" and "Old MacDonald" are two suggestions. Old MacDonald is a sequential song when each animal is repeated in every verse. Children need to be 3½ or 4 before they can do this. Other sequence songs:

> There's a Hole in My Bucket
> The Twelve Days of Christmas
> The Farmer's in his den
> She'll Be Comin' 'Round the Mountain

4. Use a drum (or a pot and a wooden spoon) to teach concepts of fast and slow, loud and soft. Let children move to the drum beat as you hit the drum first quickly, then slowly. Ask children to clap their hands or stamp their feet accordingly as you hit the drum loudly and softly.

5. Play music that has a story or suggests a certain idea, for example, "Morning" from the *Peer Gynt Suite* by Edvard Grieg. Talk about the morning, listening to the birds, feeling the sun on your face, etc. Then play the music and let children move freely to the music, or draw what they "see" in the music.

6. Using rhythm instruments, play a game with children that gives them an opportunity to express their feelings. Put out several rhythm instruments that have contrasting sounds, for example, bells, wood blocks, maracas, slide whistle, castanets, tambourine. Say to the children, "When I awoke this morning, I felt like _____". Ask them to choose an instrument with a sound that corresponds to how they felt this morning. Encourage them to play it and describe their feeling. Play all the instruments with the children and find words to describe the sounds of the instrument—happy, sad, excited, angry, scared, etc.

The I Can't Sing Book

7. Draw pictures to illustrate the lyrics of a song. For example, hold up pictures of each finger as the children sing "Where Is Thumbkin?" During the last verse "Where's the whole family?" hold up pictures the children have made of the outlines of their own hands. Other songs that are easy to find illustrations for are "The Old Lady Who Swallowed a Fly", "Five Little Monkeys" and "The Wheels on the Bus". These musical games are visually stimulating and develop thinking skills.

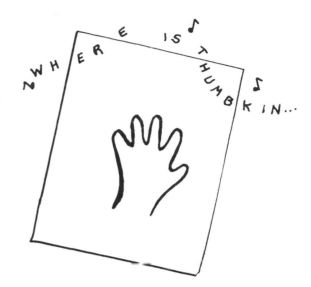

8. Pass out rhythm sticks of various colours to the children. Rhythm sticks usually come in primary colours. Ask the children to hold them in their laps. Sing or play a familiar song such as "Twinkle, Twinkle, Little Star". Hold up a colour card (for example, blue) and those children with blue sticks hold them in the air and pretend to conduct. Put down the blue card, and the children with blue sticks put them down. Hold up another card of a different colour. This game teaches colour identification and matching and develops gross motor skills.

9. If you have access to a piano or an autoharp, you have a simple science lesson right at your fingertips, and you don't even have to know how to play. Pluck the largest, thickest string; watch it vibrate. Pluck the smallest, shortest string; you can hear the high sound but cannot see it move, because it is vibrating very fast. This is how sound is produced, through the movement of air. Another experiment shows vibration with a rubber band. Stretch it. The tighter you stretch the rubber band, the higher its sound when plucked; the looser you stretch it, the lower the sound. This is a visual and auditory experience of how sound is produced.

10. Make your own wind chimes by hanging nails from a string. Attach different sized nails to a long piece of twine or rope by tying a piece of string around each nail and then tying it on the twine or rope. Hang the twine (with the nails attached) to a tree branch. Listen to the music when the wind blows.

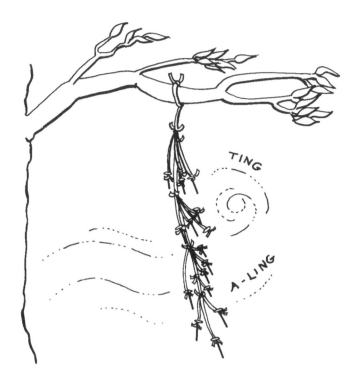

11. Hold your palm in front of your face and blow air into your hand. As you are blowing the air, take your other hand's index finger and move it up and down through the blowing air. You will be able to hear the sound of the air change.

12. Sing directions all day long—for transitions (putting things away), for mealtime, for bedtime, etc.

13. Sing the following to the tune of "Are You Sleeping?"

> Hello Brian, hello Brian
> Where are you? Where are you?
> I'm so glad you're with us.
> I'm so glad you're with us.
> How are you, how are you?

Brian answers "Here I am." This is also a great way for children to learn each other's name. If you have a child who does not want to participate, walk over to that child and sing the answer for him.

The I Can't Sing Book

14. Find out each child's favourite song and write it down next to the child's name on a chart. When you sing that particular song, point out whose favourite song it is. This is an excellent way to develop positive self-concept in young children. What you are saying to the child is, "your opinion is important".

15. Sing a lullaby with children. Let each child hold a favourite doll or stuffed animal. As you sing, let them rock their dolls. Some nice lullabies are "Hush Little Baby" and "Rock a Bye Baby" (see pages 14–16 for more suggestions).

16. Sing (or say) counting songs and poems such as "Five Little Monkeys", "This Old Man", and "One, Two, Buckle My Shoe".

17. Fill the same-size water glasses to different heights. Tap them on the sides with a spoon and listen for the difference in the sound. Which is lower? higher?

18. Tap the same water glasses two ways. Tap them with your finger in the water and then with no finger in the water.

Music Is...A Great Way to Teach

19. Watch another person or persons playing musical instruments, or invite an older child or an adult who plays an instrument to come to your class and play for the children.

20. Have a good old-fashioned sing-along with lots of clapping, stamping and fun. What a wonderful way to start the day!

The I Can't Sing Book

chapter 10

• Music Is...
Classical

•

Music by the great masters is inspiring and invigorating; it affects our emotions, relieves stress and appeals to our innate sense of beauty. Introducing children to classical music and helping them appreciate it is a wonderful and meaningful gift. The following selections provide a variety of experiences for young children. They stimulate imagination (*Carnival of the Animals*), tell a story (*Surprise Symphony*), encourage dramatic play (*Flight of the Bumblebee*), provide movement opportunities (*The Nutcracker*) and have many musical styles and rhythms.

Some additional suggestions that young children love are:

Moonlight Sonata, First Movement

LUDWIG VAN BEETHOVEN

What can you do in the moonlight besides sleep? Great for
pretending.

Hansel and Gretel

ENGELBERT HUMPERDINCK (NOT THE SINGER)

This story is a Grimm's Fairy Tale about a witch who lures two young
children to her gingerbread house. It can be a little scary for young
children; use your judgment.

Wedding March from Lohengrin

RICHARD WAGNER

"Here Comes the Bride" with an orchestra. Children love this.

Minute Waltz

FREDERICK CHOPIN

Watch the clock and see if this really takes a minute to play. It has
been said that if you omit the repeats, it can be played in 48 seconds.
You can also do aerobic exercise to this music for one minute.

William Tell Overture

GIOACCHINO ROSSINI

Very familiar music and the children can pretend to ride on horses.
This was the theme from the "Lone Ranger" television show years
ago.

Pomp and Circumstance

SIR EDWARD ELGAR

The title comes from Shakespeare's *Othello*. You will recognize this
famous music.

The Blue Danube

JOHANN STRAUSS

Infectious music that you have to dance to.

The I Can't Sing Book

Knightsbridge

ERIC COATES

Eric Coates was born in the small mining town of Hucknall near Nottingham in 1886, the son of a doctor. He learnt to play a violin at the age of six, and although his parents wanted him to work in a bank, he loved music so much that he went to London at the age of 20 to study at the Royal Academy of Music. Although always a country man, he spent a large part of his life in London and his two London Suites reflect the various aspects of city life as no other composer has done. He composed the Knightsbridge March whilst walking through the streets of London, and he had in his mind great multitudes of people all walking. This may account for the brisk tempo.

Movement

Play Knightsbridge and march to the music. Imagine that you are in a crowd of commuters marching to work. Other famous marches by Eric Coates are *Oxford Street*, and *Calling all Workers*.

Clair de Lune

CLAUDE DEBUSSY

Claude Debussy was a French composer whose music is called "impressionistic". If you've seen impressionistic paintings (Monet, Degas), you know that the pictures often look like a photo that is out of focus. Impressionistic music sounds fuzzy with soft sounds and dreamy melodies. *Clair de Lune* is music that describes the moonlight.

Art

Make a moon with yellow construction paper.

Movement

Listen to the music and dance around the room holding your moon in the air. When the music is over, lie down and pretend to go to sleep.

Music is...Classical

Flight of the Bumblebee 3+

NIKOLAY RIMSKY-KORSAKOV

This piece is a vivid musical description of the insect's flight and is an excellent demonstration of how music can imitate life. Play the music and listen for the fast and slow movement of the bumblebee.

Art

Make simple paper wings. Attach them to the shirt backs with Velcro and pretend to be bumblebees flying around as you listen to the music.

Drama

Pretend to be bumblebees and fly around the room. Land on flowers, sip the nectar and fly some more.

Nutrition

Enjoy honey with bread or biscuits.

Rodeo 3+

AARON COPLAND

Aaron Copland is an American composer whose music reflects America. He is best known for his use of cowboy and American folk songs in his music. The Shaker hymn "Simple Gifts" is the main theme of his piece *Appalachian Spring*. In the composition called *Rodeo* there is a section called Hoe-down. Listen to the music and point out the fiddles.

Movement

Dance to the music and let your child move freely in any way that she chooses.

The I Can't Sing Book

Language

Use "square dance" talk as you dance around with your child.

> Swing your partner
> Do si do around the room
> Round and around with your best gal or guy

I bet you can think of some more "square dance" language.

Symphony No. 5 in C minor 3+

LUDWIG VAN BEETHOVEN

The amazing thing about Beethoven was that he began to go deaf at age 26. He was able to hear his music in his mind and he composed some of his greatest works at the end of his life when he was completely deaf.

Language

The first movement of this symphony is very famous and it is fun to make up words to the familiar four notes that are heard over and over. Some ideas for words are "knock at the door" (knock on a table or door), "my name is John", "happy new year". Whatever words you decide on using, each time you hear those four notes, say the words. Little children really enjoy playing this game and will remember this music forever.

Carnival of the Animals 3+

CAMILLE SAINT-SAËNS

This is a very humorous piece of music that uses different instruments to imitate the elephant, kangaroo, cuckoo, lion, swan and other animals. Play the piece one section at a time talking about the animal that the music is describing. The notes on the cassette or CD will probably tell you what instrument is being used to portray the particular animal.

Movement

When you have listened to two or three sections, try to imitate the
   animals as you listen to the music.
Pretend to be a Jack in the Box and each time you hear the "cuckoo"
   in the music, pop up out of your box.
Move like a swan swimming in the water. Now, listen to the music and
   pretend to be a swan.

Language

Listen to the "cuckoo". Ask your child to make the "cuckoo" sound
   every time he hears it in the music.
Talk about swans before you listen to the music. Look at pictures and
   read the story "The Ugly Duckling" by Hans Christian Anderson.

Surprise Symphony, 2nd movement   3+

FRANZ JOSEF HAYDN

Haydn was affectionately called "Papa Haydn" because he was very
   helpful to young composers. He was known for his wonderful
imagination and sense of humour. Many stories have been told about
this music. One such anecdote said that Haydn put in the loud chord
   to wake up the people who were sleeping at the concert.

The I Can't Sing Book

Language

You will recognize the melody in this piece of music. Children love to play this game. First, tell the following story:

Papa Hadyn Story

JACKIE SILBERG

Once upon a time there was a man named Mr Haydn. He worked very hard at his job. His job was composing (writing beautiful music for other musicians to play on their instruments). One day, while Papa Haydn was working very hard he began to get sleepy and he fell fast asleep in a chair. When his children came into the room and saw that he was sleeping, they decided to play a funny trick on him. First they were very quiet and tiptoed around the room and then, all of a sudden, they made a lot of noise and jumped up and down. Of course, Papa Haydn woke up and was very surprised. He thought that it was a funny joke, so he wrote some music about what had happened.

Now play the second movement of the *Surprise Symphony*. You will know when the surprise comes. Say the following poem in a soft voice either with the music or by itself.

Papa Haydn

Papa Haydn's gone to sleep. (pretend to be sleeping)
He told his children, "Don't make a peep." (keep sleeping)
But they were such naughty boys,
And they made a LOT OF NOISE. (say the words in a loud voice and jump up and down).
　　　　　　Jackie Silberg

The Nutcracker   3+

PETER ILYITCH TCHAIKOVSKY

Tchaikovsky wrote many beautiful pieces of music that are wonderful for young children to listen to. *The Nutcracker* is very popular and is excellent for acting out.

Three selections from *The Nutcracker* are:

- "March of the Toy Soldiers"—pretend to be a toy soldier. March to the music with your legs stiff.

- "Dance of the Sugarplum Fairy"—ask your child what sweets she likes to eat. Cut out pictures of your favourite festive foods from magazines. Dance like a fairy (light on your feet) to the music. Change the name of "sugarplum" to another sweet—gumdrop fairy, M&M fairy, etc.

- "Waltz of the Flowers"—look at pictures of flowers and cut them out to make a collage. Hold flowers in your hands as you dance to the music.

- *The Sleeping Beauty* and *1812 Overture* are also excellent pieces by Tchaikovsky for listening.

The Grand Canyon Suite   4+

FERDE GROFE

Composers often find inspiration for their music in nature. *The Grand Canyon Suite* has five parts—Sunrise, Painted Desert, On the Trail, Sunset and Cloudburst. "On the Trail" is excellent for young children to listen to.

Language
Listen for the music that sounds like the clippety clopping of the mules as they climb the trail to the top of the mountain.

The I Can't Sing Book

Science and Nature

Talk about the different animals that you might see along the trail. They include deer, squirrels, porcupines, snakes and mountain lions. It is also interesting to notice that cactus grows at the bottom of the canyon and tall fir trees grow at the top. Talk about how weather and climate affect plants.

Sounds of Nature in Music

Many natural sounds are musical. The sound of wind rustling the leaves as it passes through a tree, the song of a lark, the rhythmic chirping of crickets, even the soft sounds of snow falling—all of these sounds have rhythm; some of them even have pitch. No wonder composers of some of the finest music in the world have been inspired by the sounds of nature! Here are some examples that you can play for your children.

Four Seasons

ANTONIO VIVALDI

Imitates a thunderstorm in the Summer Concerto.

Sixth Symphony

LUDWIG VAN BEETHOVEN

The last movement imitates thunderstorms.

The Grand Canyon Suite

FERDE GROFE

Music depicts the wonders of nature, including sunrises.

Animals Sounds in Music

Concerto in D Major for Flute and Orchestra

ANTONIO VIVALDI

Depicts the goldfinch.

Wolf Eyes

PAUL WINTER

Juxtaposes the howl of a real wolf with the imitative "howl" of a saxophone.

Peter and the Wolf

SERGEI PROKOFIEV

Demonstrates various instruments of the orchestra while imitating the following animal sounds: bird—flute; duck—oboe; wolf—horns; cat—clarinet. If you feel that this story is too violent, change the ending by catching the wolf and taking him to the zoo.

Science and Nature

Go for a walk at different times of the year. Listen for all kinds of sounds. Take a tape recorder and record all of the sounds you hear. Label the tapes Spring, Summer, Autumn and Winter or label them for the month during which the tapes were recorded. Play the tapes at different times of the year and recall the different sounds.

Purchasing and Taking Care of Music

With the vast selection of available music, knowing what to buy and how to take care of it is very important. It is important to have quality equipment to play your music on. Your children deserve the best.

Purchasing Music

There are three choices for purchasing music for listening.

> CDs (compact discs)
> Cassette tapes
> LP records

Compact discs (CDs) are the best source of recorded music. You can choose the songs on the CD you want played, and you can program a CD player to play the same song over and over. This is very convenient when you want to learn or teach a song. Compact discs are more durable than cassettes.

Cassette tapes are portable, small and lightweight. You can play a cassette in the car or anywhere else that has a cassette tape player. Playing cassettes in a car makes driving with a young child a pleasant experience.

LPs are pretty much outdated these days with the popularity of CD players. The advantage of using a record (if you don't have a CD player) is that you can always choose the song that you want to play.

Taking Care of Music

● Both compact discs and cassette tapes should not be exposed to very hot or cold temperatures.
● Keep compact discs and cassette tapes in their cases. They will last longer and get extra protection.

Research shows that using music and movement together or using language and movement together uses both sides of the brain.

chapter 11

• Questions Frequently Asked

by Parents · and Teachers

•

Do you have a musical genius at your house? Do your children get wild when they hear loud and fast music? When is the right time to start music lessons? You will find some answers to these questions and more in the following section.

Q. We have a box of rhythm instruments in our classroom containing a drum, some sticks, a triangle and a maraca. The children fight to play the drum and ignore the other instruments. What should we do?

A. Children should be familiar with the instruments that are available in the classroom. Try introducing one instrument at a time, one a day, or one a week, whichever fits best into your schedule. Start with a maraca, for example.

1. Ask the children to sit in a circle.
2. Show the maraca and explain how to play it. Then, say its name and ask the children to repeat the name after you.
3. Give the maraca to the first child. The child examines the instrument, plays it, says its name and passes it to the next child.
4. The instrument is passed around the circle. Each child gets to feel it, play it, say its name.
5. Next time, introduce a different instrument. Soon, the children will know about each one of the instruments and may no longer "play favourites".

Q. I have a child who absolutely refuses to sing with the group. What is your advice?

A. The most important thing to remember is to respect the child's decision not to sing. The child may have very legitimate reasons for not singing. Just because a child is not singing does not mean he is not participating. He is still hearing and learning the songs. You may gently attempt to get the child to participate by letting him do an activity that goes with the song. He could wave a flag if the song is patriotic, or beat a drum to the rhythm. If there are no activities that go with the song, try having the child sit on your lap while you and the class sing the song. This way, he'll be surrounded by the music. Above all, do not try to force the child to sing.

Q. At what age should a parent or teacher encourage a child to begin music lessons?

A. Musical experiences can begin at a very early age. Playing music in the home or at school, taking children to music events and singing with children will encourage and enhance their musical development. It is best, however, because of motor development, to start formal music lessons at age eight or nine.

IMPORTANT: Do not force the child to take music lessons! This may cause a negative reaction to music. If the child has been exposed to music in early childhood, it is likely that he will ask the parent for lessons.

Q. What are the differences between all the different musical teaching methods? I'm confused.

A. I understand your confusion. A brief description of music methods follows.

Suzuki—a music teaching method that originated in Japan. It was founded by Shinichi Suzuki, born in 1898, who possessed a profound love of music and children. This method is based on the "mother-tongue" method of imitation and rote learning that parallels that of acquiring language skills at an early age. Children can start Suzuki lessons in piano and violin as young as age three. Through the creative and intelligent use of Suzuki's philosophy and method, we can help children develop both technique and musicianship to an astoundingly high level.

Orff-Schulwerk—bases its music teaching on the things that children like to do: singing, chanting, rhyming, clapping and dancing. Children are encouraged to participate at their own level. It is a child-centred process. Playing musical instruments is also a vital part of the Orff-Schulwerk method. The instruments include tuned drums, xylophones, metallophones, glockenspiels and recorders.

Kodaly Method—a vocal approach to music based on Hungarian folk literature. This music education programme evolved in Hungary in the 1930s under the guidance of the composer and musicologist Zoltan Kodaly. Singing, listening, movement, ear training and creating are developed at every level starting with preschool.

Gordon Learning Theory—Edwin E. Gordon is a music researcher known for his tests to measure musical aptitude. He believes that music follows the same progression as language development and he uses that as a basis for his ideas in inference and discrimination learning.

Dalcroze—Emile Jaques-Dalcroze formulated a comprehensive philosophy of music teaching through creative movement that is called "eurhythmics". Children listen to piano music and respond with their bodies. Many professional musicians have had Dalcroze training.

Q. Whenever I hear a new song that I would like to teach, I have trouble remembering the melody. Any suggestions?

A. Learning the words and music at the same time can be overwhelming. One solution to your problem is to use a tape recorder to play the song. Sing along with the recording as you teach the song to children. If that doesn't work, try this method: Learn the words first, then try to learn the melody. This may make the process easier. If, in the end, you simply can't remember the melody, make up your own melody, and sing it with confidence! After all, it is the enjoyment of the song and the interaction with children that is important—not the "professional" version of the song.

Q. Sometimes children become so stimulated that I have a hard time settling them down. How would you handle this?

A. Just as music can stimulate, it can be used to calm. Try ending with a quiet song, or sing a song slowly and softly. Another suggestion is to sing a familiar song using finger motions, such as "Two Little Blackbirds", "Where Is Thumbkin?", "Open, Shut Them" or "Incy Wincy Spider".

The I Can't Sing Book

Sing the song a few times, each time more slowly. The children will concentrate on the actions while your calm, soothing voice settles them down.

Q. Sarah is very talented musically. What can I do to encourage and develop her talent?

A. You are obviously providing a wonderful musical environment for Sarah or you wouldn't have recognized this talent. Surround Sarah with musical opportunities. Have simple rhythm instruments around the house, watch musical programmes on television and take Sarah to concerts. By providing these opportunities, you will be creating an environment that will nurture her talent. You might consult with local music teachers as to the best time to start lessons. For example, if a child studies voice before her vocal cords have matured, it could damage her voice. An expert voice teacher will know these details.

Q. I would love to play a musical instrument (I've never had any lessons), but I'm afraid I might be too old to learn. Do you have any advice for me?

A. Unless you have a physical disability that would prevent you from holding or playing an instrument, you can learn to play an instrument at any age. If you have a desire to play a musical instrument, why not take lessons? The rewards will be worth the effort! Group classes are often a good way to start.

Q. I would like to introduce my child to classical music, but he seems more interested in rock and roll. What shall I do?

A. Try to acquaint your child with classical music gradually. Try "Brahms Lullaby" at night-time or "The Nutcracker" at Christmas. Also, don't neglect the music of today's fine children's artists. Many of these artists perform their songs in a manner that combines many musical styles, including classical.

Q. What is the best time of day to have a music period?

A. A specific music period enables you to pursue specific music goals such as learning about rhythm or sounds, or learning songs. It is also an effective teaching technique to use music throughout the day for transition times, language development and pure enjoyment. If you want to have a specific music period each day, first thing in the morning or late afternoon works very well.

Q. We have a Show-and-Tell period. The children sometimes bring certain pop recordings. If I play the recordings, the children become very excited, dance and are often out of control. How should I handle this?

A. This can be handled in several ways. If you simply cannot manage the children during a period like this, then you should send a note to the parents, asking them not to let the children bring these recordings to Show-and-Tell. Another method is to schedule the Show-and-Tell period so that it takes place before outside play. This way, the children can let off steam outside. The third suggestion is to ration this kind of activity to once a month or so. Again, try to schedule Show-and-Tell time so that it precedes outdoor play.

Q. How can we incorporate music into our infant and toddler programme?

A. First of all, remember to sing often. Children love to be sung to regardless of the quality of your voice. Pick up each child, hold him close and dance gently as you sing. Naturally, every child gets a turn. Play singing games like "Peek-a-boo", "This Little Piggie" and "To Market, To Market". Play soothing music from CDs or cassette tapes at appropriate times. As you know, there are many wonderful children's recordings on the market. In fact, most of today's children's music is far superior musically to much of the music you can find on the radio. Rock the babies and sing lullabies.

The I Can't Sing Book

Glossary

Accent—an emphasis given to certain musical notes (tones).

Band—brass, percussion and woodwind instruments that play together. There are military bands, jazz bands, dance bands and brass bands. Usually there are no string instruments in a band.

Beat—a repeated rhythmic pulse; the rhythm you respond to in dancing or marching.

Bell—objects that make clinking sounds.

Call and response—alternating between a single voice and a group of voices, usually with the response (the group) singing the same thing as the call (the single voice).

Castanets—clappers usually made out of wood and held in the hands, played by striking the castanet with a finger creating a clicking sound.

Chant—a group of words spoken rhythmically.

Chord—three or more musical notes (tones) played at the same time.

Chorus—a group of voices that sing together; also the part of a song that repeats between verses.

Classical music—sometimes called exact music. The composer wanted the music played exactly like it was written without improvisation. This term also means the exact music of the 18th and early 19th century.

Composer—someone who writes (composes) music.

Conductor—the leader of a group of musicians who play music together.

Crescendo—a group of notes that gradually become louder.

Cymbals—a percussion instrument made out of a thin concave disc of bronze that is held at the centre so that the edges are free to vibrate. Striking the cymbal makes it sound with a loud crash.

Decrescendo—a group of notes that gradually become softer.

Drum—a percussion instrument that has a base with a stretched skin across the top. The tightness of the skin determines whether the sound will be high or low when struck with a stick.

Fingerplays—hand, finger and arm movements suggested by the words of a song or poem.

Folk songs—songs handed down from one generation to another; usually the composer is unknown.

Hand jive—expressing music with your hands or body.

Harmony—two or more tones sounding at the same time.

Instruments—anything that makes music or accompanies music, including the voice.

Kazoo—a simple instrument that makes a buzzing sound when you hum or sing into it.

Lullaby—a gentle song that makes you feel like rocking back and forth, usually soothing and relaxing.

Lyrics—the words of a song.

Maracas—a pair of gourds filled with dry seeds and shaken rhythmically to accompany music.

Melody—the succession of musical tones moving up or down in a musical composition.

Meter—a basic grouping of beats. Groupings can be in two, three, four, six or more beats.

Metronome—a mechanical device that keeps a steady beat, marking the tempo of a composition.

Musical notes—the individual tones of music.

Musician—someone who makes music.

Orchestra—brass, woodwinds, strings and percussion instruments that make up an orchestra.

Percussion instruments—generic term for instruments that are sounded by shaking or striking one object with another.

Phrase—a musical thought just like a sentence in language.

Pitch—the high or low sound of a music note.

Recorder—a vertical flute with finger holes and a mouthpiece like a whistle.

Rest—the quiet between the notes; the silence between the sound.

Rhythm—a pattern that repeats itself over and over.

Rhythm instruments—the same as percussion instruments.

Sand blocks—tone blocks with sandpaper on the backs of the blocks, played by scraping the blocks together.

Scale—tones that follow a pattern going upward (ascending) or downward (descending).

Shaker—any percussion instrument that makes sounds when shaken.

Stanza—a group of lines of music. Usually four lines. Also called a verse.

Symphony—music written for an orchestra usually in four parts. An orchestra is also called a symphony.

Tambourine—a small circular drum with jingles set into the frame for shaking or hitting.

Tempo—speed at which music is played.

Tone—the sound of a definite pitch. A tone can be long or short, soft or loud.

Tone blocks—handheld wooden blocks of different lengths, played by hitting with a wooden stick.

Triangle—a steel bar shaped into a triangle, played by striking with a steel beater.

Xylophone—a tuned percussion instrument with bars or bells of different sizes graduated in length to sound a scale when struck with a wooden stick (mallet).

The I Can't Sing Book

Index

Other books by Jackie Silberg

available from Brilliant Publications

Games to Play With Babies

Games to Play With Toddlers

Games to Play With Two Year Olds